6th Dimensional Thinking

2nd Mezreth book

Steve Strong + Lea Kapiteli

Publication details

6th Dimensional Thinking
BY STEVE STRONG
LEA KAPITELI

© 2024 Printed in Australia.
All characters and events in this book are based on factual people and happenings from around the world and beyond. Any resemblance of these characters and events from other media sources is purely coincidental.

This book is protected under the copyright laws of Australia. Any reproduction or unauthorized use of material or artwork contained within this book is prohibited without the express permission from the author and/or publication.

The author and/or publication has not authorized any sales of this book without its cover and/or publication page. If you procured this copy of the book without a cover, then the author and/or publisher has not received payment for this copy.

Printed and distributed by IngramSpark
https://www.ingramspark.com/

Illustrations by Lea Kapiteli.

Cover design by Erica Schmerbeck & Lea Kapiteli

This edition was initially printed as a paperback cover.

About the Authors

Steve Strong is a secondary school teacher with a background in Archaeology and Education. He was involved in the formation of a Graduate Diploma of Aboriginal Education for the N.S.W. Department of Education, writing units on Traditional Law and Contemporary History. He also co-authored the highly successful "Aboriginal Australia: A Language and Cultural kit".

Evan Strong has a background in Anthropology & Indigenous Cultural Studies, Counselling & Mediation with a Bachelor's Degree in Social Sciences and Graduate Studies in Psychology. Evan has worked as a researcher for the Northern Rivers Area Health Service, a Social Worker, Teachers Aide.

Lea Kapiteli was born in New Zealand in 1993 into a Croatian family that migrated to Australia in 1998. But, more importantly: she has been in psychic contact with extra-terrestrials and extra-dimensionals since early childhood, even recalls some of her past lives and the numbing existence beyond life.

Steve's Chapter	1
Lea's Chapter	10
Transcript Twelve Chapter 23	19
Transcript Thirteen Chapter 24	25
Transcript Fourteen Chapter 25	31
Transcript Fifteen Chapter 26	39
Transcript Sixteen Chapter 27	47
Transcript Seventeen Chapter 28	55
Transcript Eighteen Chapter 29	61
Transcript Nineteen Chapter 30	67
Transcript Twenty Chapter 31	75
Transcript Twenty-one Chapter 32	81
Transcript Twenty-two Chapter 33	93
Transcript Twenty-three Chapter 34	99
Transcript Twenty-four Chapter 36	105
Transcript Twenty-five Chapter 38	111
Blended Answers	118
Transcript One Chapter 12	165
Transcript Two Chapter 13	171
Transcript Three Chapter 14	179
Transcript Four Chapter 15	185
Transcript Five Chapter 16	193
Transcript Six Chapter 17	201
Transcript Seven Chapter 18	211
Transcript Eight Chapter 19	221
Transcript Nine Chapter 20	233
Transcript Ten Chapter 21	241
Transcript Eleven Chapter 22	249
Lea's Final Comments	258
Conclusion	260

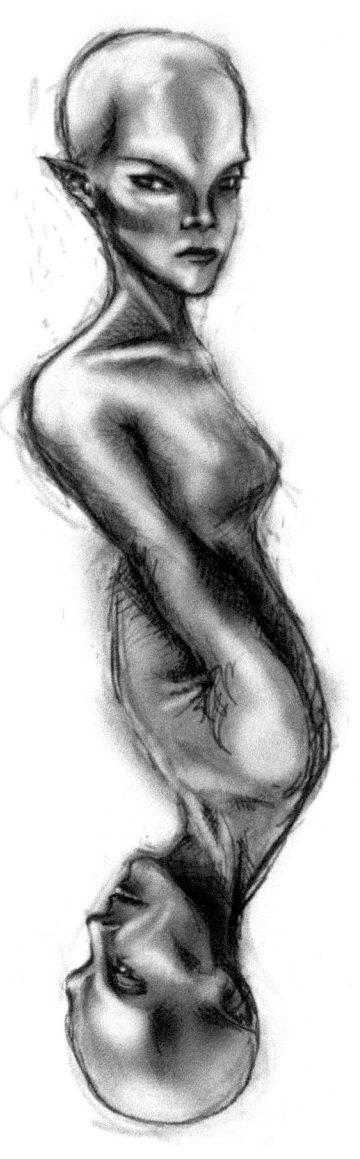

This book was indirectly written by Mezreth. Using the questions Steven has asked throughout the transcripts, all Mezreth's answers are connected to each other. You will notice that there are repetitive answers and questions, so, don't worry if you're accidentally rereading the same thing twice!

In these coming pages, there will be identical questions, but paired with slightly different answers. However, when you paste them together, you will notice that these answers are whole. What's more astounding, that these answers were given at different times.

If you strip these words of their questions and put them altogether, order them in a way to make sense, they tell of a grander picture. It adds to the notion that Mezreth does not operate in a linear chronological reality as we do, some may say,

it's sixth dimensional thinking.

Steve's Chapter

There are three principal areas of research in this book, which we believe are all unique. It is our contention that the retrieval, setting and supplier of content are lacking in comparison or precedents. The insights, observations and recommendations are given by an off world being that under normal conditions can never die, ever. The actual words relayed through Lea, who acts as an interlocutor, is gathered through an utterly subjective process that is totally lacking in any empirical science.

What Lea does, has nothing to do with channelling and is more a symbolic interpretation/discussion. There are no theatrics, grunts, changes in voice or physical contortions; it is just a question-and-answer session, where more often than not, most of my questions are rarely directly addressed yet always responded to, but only as he sees fit.

In our First book (Interview with an Alien) Lea went into considerable detail explaining how her relationship with Mezreth came about, and if the reader needs more evidence, we recommend reading that book. Nevertheless, I do intend to offer two brief observations that give some credence to her being in actual contact with this extremely important Alien.

From the time we first saw Lea give a presentation detailing the personalities and roles of certain off-world beings she made contact with, as convincing her talk and general demeanour was, my empirical radar demanded more proof. The ten questions I asked Lea, began as being something that could be known and concluded with two questions no-one but myself could answer. They were incredibly personal, and the last two answers were not known by the closest person to me, my wife. After the tenth question, I realised it became pointless going further, but even so there still have been momentary lapses in faith where my doubts began to return, but on each occasion, I would read some of the transcripts. That was enough; the breadth of subjects and unwavering quality of insight in replies was well past the capacity of not only Lea, but any Earthly human resident.

And it is that one recurring truth I would suggest the reader will come to appreciate. It all comes down to an inescapable truth, either Mezreth or Lea is speaking, there is no-one else on the podium. To assist each reader in determining who is the being speaking, I did ask Lea about her time and progress in secondary schooling. The logic is if Lea is the source, surely such intellectual prowess would be clearly on show at school? Her report card was a story of little effort, there were no outstanding marks or essays and upon leaving high school she did not continue further academic study.

What you will find when reading Mezreth's responses is the incredible contextual spread of topics and issues addressed. We intend to present and analyse what he said using two different approaches. As before in the first book, we will once again provide every question asked and reply given in transcript form, but due to a cardinal mistake I made in compiling the questions there is now another 'big picture' path to tread.

What happened recently, in fact the gap in timing was nine weeks, was that I mistakenly sent to Lea a set of questions already asked. Neither of us originally picked up the unintended repetition, although Lea did start to wonder during the reading. It was only apparent after we compared his answers given then to those before, and what shocked us was in nearly every second answer there was an extension or rearrangement on what was first said. Sometimes the opening sentence was identical, or close to it, but past that it was always an extension. Upon looking and comparing elsewhere, it became clear that this was the norm, and this prompted us to mix and match.

What that realisation of extensions throughout lead onto was the cutting of all his printed comments into hundreds and hundreds of thin slips of paper. All up, there are twelve categories, and all we had to do was find the correct heading then work out an order, so that the passages connected and flowed as seamlessly as possible. On occasions I had to add a few words ranging up to a longer sentence, so that the link was clear. In most cases there was little addition needed, as it was clear Mezreth was deliberately adding or extending on what was said months earlier.

Our rationale in compiling general concepts to follow on after the section including each question alongside the specific answer was to provide two paths to pursue, one giving a 'big picture' and the second approach is a more concise examination of one small piece of advice.

In combination Mezreth is sharing so much information to assist each soul to be able to understand that the ceremony that took place at Uluru just over three years ago, has led to the successful beginning of a process of ascension which will eventually transform the planet. With the exception of humans, all other animals will be part of this global change in circumstances and vibrations, people alone must earn and deserve to be given 'a ticket to ride.'

To do so, the information and guidance Mezreth shares is all you need to pay the 'price of admission,' or maybe it is all just made-up stories and bogus advice given by Lea. It is one or the other, as there is no third choice or protagonist.

This chapter contains the set of questions that was accidentally asked twice. After each question we have supplied Mezreth's first response followed by his second response given to the same question asked two months later.

1. Dolores Cannon is adamant that "ETs are living now on the Earth, they are everywhere among your friends, neighbours and even relatives. Their blood flows through our veins, we are as much brothers and sisters to beings from the stars as we are to the animals of the Earth." What is fascinating is that Dolores makes no distinction between Mezreth, us and all types of animals, is she correct? Does that mean we have all incarnated into different animal forms in previous lives?

First Response: A soul has no race, gender, species or ego. All are the same and all are Akashi.

Second Response: Soul has no species, race or sex. Soul is soul. You would be surprised at what runs in our veins if you look a little deeper.

2. Dolores extends not only the participants but localities in claiming "through reincarnation we come and go to different locations, earth is merely a school." Does that mean nearly all, if not all, present-day human residents have incarnated in other constellations? And does this school, which you have often said it is one of the most difficult schools in the Cosmos to learn from, have the most taxing subjects in this Earthly curriculum?

First Response: All life is a school. It gives us the tools to understand purpose, and through purpose we gain meaning to existence. Each life is with unique challenges, but it is up to the soul how difficult they wish to make it for themselves. Hardships can breed heroes or ghosts. Earth is one of many, many places, but it shares this cycle of strife with very few worlds. For that alone, it must be guarded.

Second Response: All life is a school. Life will test your buoyancy in water-no matter what, but if you wish to prove you are a strong swimmer, go where you may drown.

3. While deposited in the realm of difficult challenges, our religious beliefs are such a tortuous path to travel. We have religions and sects/cults who believe their teachings exclusively guarantee admission to 'heaven'. Followers, if instructed by their leader will commit suicide or mass genocide of unbelievers and believe such atrocities will gain God's approval and endorsement. The many inquisitions sanctioned every type of torture and depravity but was done so firmly convinced it was approved by God. They carried out warfare slaughtering women and children, and even after doing the most heinous acts of depravity genuinely believed if they confessed and feigned contrition God would forgive any indiscretion, and so it continues. Do other Alien civilisations match this diversity in beliefs in relation to what the Creator will approve, or are their understandings of life, death and ascension more consistent, compassionate and uniform?

First Response: My kin invented religion. In our innocence and ignorance, we believed you would benefit from it in those early days. We were proven wrong. Religion does not suit you now, like it suited others. We hoped that it would best teach you how to be in service to the Universe, but the angry and hurt few, saw this service and warped it to serve themselves. You are young, I know you see religion as an enemy ... but its intention was to give you a set of skills that could have helped you evolve.

Second Response: Every act or inaction serves the next life you need to lead. Most doctrines make this very clear, but it's rarely practised. Just as rare as love. Humans can create any excuse to slaughter each other, using religion as a civilised excuse to behave like the devil. Make no mistake, my friend, many species have this monster inside them. The Raivan would set their families and clans ablaze if they were forbidden from practising their beliefs; the Xannians used to throw their out-dated elderly in deep sand holes and let the sun pull every drop of water from their bodies. And the Zanashj recrafted the flesh of heretics into fine chairs, tables, and other upholstery. When love and hate meet in battle, it turns us all into savages.

4. We want to pursue a topic raised in our previous Q and A in relation to animals and our relationship with them. At the supposed top end of the 'soul-pecking order,' what is the difference between the soul of a dolphin and human?

First and Second Response: None.

5. Trees do communicate, but do they also have an independent soul or spirit?

First Response: The absence of soul is the absence of life.

Second Response: All life has soul.

6. But what about ants and bees, is their soul a collective unit, do they think and exist collectively? Is one ant similar to one flake of skin on our body?

First Response: Ants tap and the bees dance to her song.

Second Response: Every speck floats in the sea of consciousness. It varies in depth. To deny one thing possesses consciousness, makes you indeed quite shallow.

7. Scientists assure us that we use no more than 15% of our brain and that this is the norm. Is that really the case? And has it always been like this?

First Response: It's just enough for you to experience the reality you invent. Anymore, you would be naked to the Universe before your time.

Second Response: The brain is a tool that can be extended with the right guidance. There was a time when you could do far more than what you do now, but these current limitations are a secret blessing—are they not?

8. How much more could we access and what capacities lay dormant inside the unused section of the brain?

First Response: You already have the power to do it all, you just lack the training.

Second Response: It can be learnt, this is true, but why do you want more? You have what you are meant to have, and it is expected of you to make the most of it.

9. Do all other animals use so little of their brain or is it running at full capacity?

First Response: They have little more than you, but only because it was granted by the Grandmother.

Second Response: Theirs is greater than yours.

10. Is that lack of engagement with so much of the largest organ in our body the fundamental block to our ascension? Is that always meant to be so, and will it continue like this after the planet transforms and ascends?

First Response: The block of your ascension is your wilful ignorance. No path has ever been impossible to travel with humility. There is no shame admitting to not knowing or being wrong, that is the key to prosperity.

Second Response: We won't give the answers before the tests come, but we can give suggestions. Ascension is earnt.

11. Let's talk about dogs, I have heard often the recent claims that dogs have taken on a new role in showing humans the path to unconditional love. Is that a valid observation?

First and Second Response: No

12. Recently my wife keeps showing me videos of dogs doing things that require the highest order of thinking, way above what scientists assume they are capable of, is that because they are now living with us and are getting smarter?

First Response: The opposite is closest to truth.

Second Response: It's the other way around.

13. And when it comes to getting smarter, human's recent track record of reality TV viewing habits and blind unquestioning obedience and acceptance, questions whether our intelligence is declining. Is this a recent descent or has it been par for the course for some time?

First Response: Our other children have created the flaws of obedience in you, casting you farther away from wisdom which was our initial plan. They conditioned you to feel contentedness when giving away your responsibility … and thereby your power. However, our other children's arrogance was a secret blessing, because it compelled you to balance the forces of your wild and wise natures. These are the keys to your salvation, but you insist on battling this ancient divide which will only lead to nothing. Yet, if you have too much of one or the other, you will be forced to restart the cycle all over again. Unfortunately, I am endless: the Earth is not.

Second Response: Excessiveness leads to indecisiveness, and indecisiveness leads to apathy, and apathy leads to laziness. If you truly want to be more intelligent, ask more, speak less, want less so you may value more.

Lea's Chapter

Mezreth is merciless once he starts speaking. He may be polite, but he won't compliment you without merit and refuses to appease your ego, even when you are in the darkest of emotional places. If you ask him something, expect only the truth, regardless of how harrowing it is. Mezreth says 'it's not about being nice, it's about keeping you honest, and the only way this can be done is being honest with yourself. I have all the time in the universe, but your life – all your years of living, disappears in a blink to me. You don't have time to waste investing in your pride, or your need for attention, or your greed, or your vanity. It is your life and ultimately your choices, but the world you inhabit is not about you. You have the opportunity few are afforded to do better, and my role is making the best out of you.'

He's been saying this to me for years in so many words, from my early teenage years to early thirties. When he and some other extra-terrestrial beings begun contact with me, I didn't understand it, I loved it at the beginning but slowly grew to resent it. The rift I felt among my peers grew into a chasm that took nearly a decade to fill. No teenager in their right mind wants to be an outcast, however, there was a time when I revelled in it. I felt unique, special, and spectacular. There was a time when I genuinely believed that everyone around me was beneath me, but unfortunately, Mezreth was watching.

To make me begin understanding, he chopped down the gnarly tree of hubris, but he left the stump there as a reminder of how bad it can become if I let it. What did he do exactly? I was becoming too indulgent on my private and personal communication with him and my other contacts. I loved being able to drift away in the higher astral planes to play with extra-terrestrial beings. I got to visit planets and stars that not even the best man-made telescopes could capture. I watched alien oceans move, sparkling clouds shift in the eerily familiar breeze and twisted lands appear as if a god had painted them with colours beyond imagining. As a teenager, I was becoming adept at harnessing these abilities into other psychic forms, telepathy being the one I loved and hated above all others.

There was something so alluring and devious being able to slip into someone's mind and co-live in their thoughts. The more I practiced, the more this gnarly tree grew in my heart. It did not take too long for this sense of superiority to reign. How could I be comparable to the mere mortals of this world; I was destined to be something glorious – I had the idea that the world will be mine. However, Mezreth was no fool. Before I could learn empathy, he ensured I was punished with it. I awoke one morning to find that my higher senses were dulled. I tried to slip into another person's mind; I was met with silence, but what followed was a stream of emotions.

When I was near someone who laughed, I couldn't hold down a chuckle and help but share their springing joy. When I was near someone who was in agony, my chest tightened, and my eyes were fighting back tears. Dear reader, I cannot understate how much I hated this, as it interfered with my ability to be around others, to consume news happening around the world and find stability within myself. However, I understand why this needed to happen and Mezreth is not shy to remind me it will happen again if that ugly tree were to sprout a fresh leaf.

If you wish to know more details about when and how our communications begun, I urge you, dear reader, to refer to our previous book, *Interview with an Alien*.

With one hand, he may be a spiritual warden and an ego-bruiser, but with the other, he offers a hand of support. In the early to mid-2010's, I was struggling with what I was meant to do with this otherworldly knowledge and experience; there were many changes to my personal life and had lost sight of what exactly I was meant to do. This plunged me into a deep depression, the kind of blackness that suppressed the ability to feel sadness – or any emotion at all. It was clear that Mezreth, nor my contacts, would command me to do anything, even when I begged them for a crumb.

'You know that's not how we do things, Lea. You need to find it on your own.' He said.

'You wanted me to be here, and you promised I won't have to be alone. You clearly want me to do something.' I said.

'Of course we want you to do something. If we didn't, then why did we bother showing you a glimpse of our lives, our worlds, and our knowledge and wisdom. Why did we bother showing you a glimpse of the greater universe through astral eyes?' He said.

'Because you said you wanted me to understand and talk about it with other people.' I said.

'You're getting closer…' he said.

'What I saw is too much to simply say! Its not something that can be done with every single person who cares about this stuff in one conversation.' I said.

'Books exist.' He said.

'But I don't know how to write one.' I said.

'Then learn how.'

This advice pulled me out of that depressive pit for quite some time. I realised writing is something I wanted to do until the day I die. It's a gift knowing what to do with one's life, and Mezreth pointed me in that direction. There was another time when I lamented how unhappy I was, and that an injection of wealth would solve all my issues (yes, I did beg Mezreth for next week's lottery numbers on several occasions and he only rolled his eyes.) He told me:

> 'If you received all those millions you lusted for, would you be happy?'

'Well, it would be a solution of many problems.' I said.

'I asked would you really be happy afterwards?' he said.

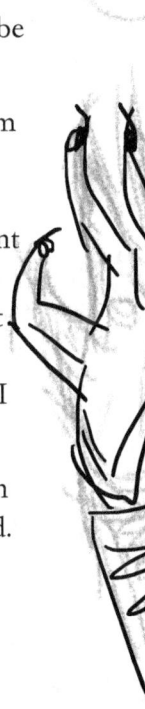

'There are many things I'm unhappy about. I wish I had more drive; I wish I was prettier, I wish for more talent and intelligence, had a better work ethic, I wish I wouldn't shut down when something didn't go the way I wanted.' I said.

'Would you treat a broken arm with a band-aid?' he said.

'No.'

'Then those issues won't be solved with money. Even if you were granted all the material wealth in the world, you wouldn't be happy – you will end up finding another thing to justify your misery. Misery and happiness are reflections of your values. Consider materials are a medium, they are used to find purpose and certainty, but many beings use them to fill empty gaps. And those gaps become the deeper as you get older if that's what you focus on.

In a previous incarnation, you had vast resources and access to things many of your peers did not, and still, you were not happy. Why? Because you value the immaterial, the things you cannot purchase or exchange away, that's why you feel miserable and that is fantastic.' He said.

'How can it be a good thing? It becomes harder to solve and it feels like I keep falling back into this pit with every reincarnation.' I said.

'And it will take you your entire life and many more lives to solve them, but at least you acknowledge it's a waste of energy to mend a broken bone with a band-aid. You can look back to see where you have come from, but you keep going.'

Despite knowing these wisdoms, it's not easy to internalise, let alone put into practice. Mezreth's most annoying trait is that he regularly reminds you of where you are wrong, but the very best part of him is how often he reminds you of how far you have come. Dear reader, everything that has been shared with me from Mezreth and my other E.T. friends have been for me when I needed to hear them. However, these words aren't relevant just to me – they belong to everyone who needs to hear them, even you.

Latest Q&A Transcripts

Transcript Twelve
Chapter 23

Steve:

According to Slater the rock engravings at Buragurra talk about Biaime coming from space and his wife Mulla Mulla not being born of the Earth but coming and returning from "on high." Is he correct?

Slater also claims Biaime means to "cut off to build," and that is why he only has one right footprint, called a Mundowa. He is virtually saying we have genes in us that are off-world; that leads towards the seminal question, did we wholly evolve on this planet without external input or are we a mixture.

This extends even further in that Slater wrote "man came to Earth with his seven senses developed." Is that true, and what are the seven senses, and if we came to earth does that imply we came here already fully evolved?

Mezreth:

Why is it written that one came from space and the other not born of us? Why not one meaning for both? If they did come from elsewhere, do you assume they were not human? If so, why make this assumption? We and humans have had a long history together and many things were shared. Some of us chose to live on earth at one point while in another time humans chose to sit by us, far away from earth. Ancient descendants still linger and wait for their young ancestors.

Both are correct.

No, none are fully or less evolved. You were just different back then.

Steve:

In this creation narrative, the men are created and put to sleep, but Numbardy (the mother) is also mentioned, but there is no inclusion of her in this long sleep. Further on Slater states that "no mention is made of the method adopted by Biaime in the making of Numbardy." Is this because it is women's business unknown to men, or is there another reason?

What is fascinating is that when the two men are woken, they were "surrounded by glorious game." However, one of the 'brothers' who is called No Name "would not kill and eat the game." He refuses to join his brother and leaves the planet. Why was this refusal to eat meat such a pivotal point?

Slater has a completely different take on what it means to be civilised. He believes we have fallen a great distance from where we began this human journey in stating that "man in the beginning of time had a higher sense of his duty to man and the development of life — which was the soul — than can be found in the cultural nations of 2,000 years ago or the nations of today." Is he right?

Original Dreaming refers to these spirits/angels as Sky-heroes, in the Bible they are called angels. Which term is correct, or are they both right?

In Dreaming stories throughout Australia mention is made of the Seven Sisters of the Pleiades coming to and walking on the land in Australia. Did this happen, why did they come and did they leave?

Mezreth:

Men have mastered to see the outer world far and clear, but the women have mastered to see the inner world, deep and whole, to see the other half. You cannot use your eyes to peek inside. You must dream.

Some must eat meat to live. Some others must eat plants to live. My kin must eat light to endure.

Slater has been given sight by the ones who have eyes.

Yes.

It was us and our little siblings. We came here long before you were conceived in the dream, but we never left. We're still here.

Steve:

According to Karno the Dreaming Story associated and engraved on Ros' Rock 1 is all about Aliens of the Goanna totem, requesting permission to land in Australia but was blocked by the human Original tribes with the totems of the Crow and Eagle leading the resistance. Until the Crow realised they should come, the Goanna could not land, but once the Crow changed sides they won this battle in the skies. Karno said that this story was engraved on that rock. Is he right?

Paul Anthony Wallis believes the Elohiem of the Bible is actually not a singular God but a plural description of extra-terrestrials coming to Earth with benevolent intentions to help. Is he right?

What comes out of this is a real blurring of the edges as to what is the difference between angels and Aliens. Could you provide some clarity as the distinction and whether there is a difference?

Dolores Cannon speaks about the Creator not having a gender as such, but being the purest manifestation of love, which she feels is the most powerful force in the Cosmos. My concern is that this word is used everywhere, we have a cardboard box that was made to carry wine bottles and on it claims the wine was made with "love and care." I hear people saying "I love playing football." I am pretty sure neither example is not really love in the purest sense. Could you provide a definition for what love really is?

Mezreth:

That was one of the most important events in your history. That event changed the course of our plans for you and the evolution of your society. That moment is greater than the fall of Atlantia.

He has been given sight by those who have eyes.

The only way to save your world is by uplifting you.

It is the acknowledgment that it is an extension of you.

Transcript Thirteen
Chapter 24

Steve:

When a human woman falls pregnant, she walks a much different path to every other female animal on this planet. All bar humans give birth unassisted, spend no time in recovery, and one day after it is business as usual. For a younger woman up until 200 years ago, giving birth was the highest cause of death. It is a very difficult and extremely painful process. Why is the birthing process so different for women to all other animals? Do Alien females elsewhere in the Universe have as much trouble as their Earth-bound sisters?

Staying on the same theme, for a woman having periods is another difficult issue, for some it is debilitating, and again any comparison to all other female animals comes up with women coming first in pain, discomfort, loss of blood and sundry side-effects. Why is yet another aspect of the reproductive systems so different and intense? And once again how does that compare to Alien females?

Are women genetically 'hot-wired' to be less aggressive, violent and war-like than males, or is there another reason?

Mezreth:

You were made poorly. Those who altered you weren't considering your comfort, but they had considered how to ensure you did not surpass the animal population nor themselves. The Zanashj did have a streak of compassion during their cruel conquest, and it was not solely Earth's curse, the Xannians, the Raivan and the Ezoni (all of these are different species who have all been their victims too.) The Zanashj are not faces of Satan. They were ignorant and young. Now, they have wizened and seek to correct the errors of their ancestors. The Zanashj do not struggle with making life from their wombs, for their malleable forms are more fluid than solid. They saw the differences between you and they, and in some ways, they kept the parts that made you different.

Remember, this is a combination of alteration and accident through poor design, bred poor design, cultivating in pain and misery. Humans are not unique in that respect. The Raivan also share the same agony. But unlike you, their pain stems from the need to reproduce than the shedding process.

When the Zanashj settled here, they needed workers and thralls. They took the men and altered them to be drastically different to women.

Steve:

My wife never wants to reincarnate as a man. By free will alone could she orchestrate that?

While remaining in the field of gender preference, it seems more and more humans are having issues with their sexual identity. Sex-changes, transsexuality and to a lesser extent homosexuality, were issues never spoken about twenty years ago. Finally, after so much persecution and much worse, being gay is no longer rampantly discriminated against. Is this fluidity and sexual freedom a sign of these times or was it more repressed in less enlightened times? The Hopi did prophesy gender uncertainty as an indicator of the Earthly transformation.

In ancient times, before farming, many societies were matrilineal in structure where women had a no less than equal say in everything. Then this changed once farms, towns, cities and armies began to flourish; was all the chaos and warfare down to women losing their voice and respect? Or was it just another symptom?

Dolores Cannon is both a female and also incredibly psychic. Her readings are always a fascinating areas to explore, and the next three questions address an area we have spoken of earlier, but it such a broad field and Dolores made one comment that did throw me. She said that when in the pause state in what many call Heaven, "here no-one is judged, no matter what circumstances of their life has been." I know there is no Peter or anyone but yourself passing judgement on your words and deeds. But Dolores seems to be saying that no-one must include you. Is that right, that no judgement is passed, even by yourself, or have I misunderstood her?

Mezreth:

That choice is up to your soul.

It's a mountain of one-million changes, all brutal and all ugly. If it is soft and comfortable, the longevity of its effects is absent. The truly enlightened care little of the package. They see no outside world because their eyes are cast inwards to the deeper universe within you. Sexes, identities, all forms of selves are not a herald of a dying society, but the herald of a new vision. If you struggle to see your kin embrace their spirit, then how can you accept us when we return?

It's a mistake to assume one was superior to the other is folly, my friend. An ancient promise was made for the masculine and feminine to share space and dominance. For a time, however, I can see the ancient wisdom, but it will falter in modern days. The only way out of this cycle is by balance. That is the only key to escape your prison.

Every action has consequences, even when you are shadow, ego, body and limitations, your true self finally returns to the surface and tries to understand what and why your old life was. If your old life has made an action that tipped the delicate balance, your soul is obligated to correct it within the next. You are not judged by anyone, but you alone will reflect, then decide.

Steve:

Dolores feels the Devil being cast down from Heaven then having dominion over the Earth is not actually true in the literal sense. She sees this as a metaphor, it was us who were cast down, "when knowledge was lost." It was "consciousness" that was lost and we, as humans created this being we named as the Devil, to excuse their failings and falling. She feels we gave an identity of Satan, so that we did not have to deal with the reasons why we fell. Is that take on the Devil correct?

Then she spoke about how we first created this Devil false-myth. She believes that "people create situations which seem to prove the existence of the Devil." She went further stating that people "believe what you want and that is what you found." So, did we create the Devil to excuse away our culpability and consequences?

Her last reading really does extend the concept of reincarnation into realms I never considered. She said that "through reincarnation through plants and animals we learn how to be in balance with Mother Earth. Once they get group thinking and unison they incarnate into Nature Spirits the like of fairies, sprites and Nature Spirits. Could she include Yowies in this group, or do they remain separate? Separate to this, do fairies exist, and if they do, what can you tell us about them?

Mezreth:

Yes.

As it was with Satan, as it was with Yahweh, as it is as it was with Ra, Seth, Odin, Ishtar, so on and so forth. All these things do have life. Their aspects are true. However, their existence is perpetuated by your deeper selves.

Yowies are the true wild men of Earth. You are what could have been if the path had been different. The spirits of nature love to play with you, but they protect the wild men from you. The spirits are older than you. Older than the wild men, older than the animals, the trees, the oceans, and the mountains. The spirits. The spirits rained on earth long before our kin created our first fire.

Transcript Fourteen
Chapter 25

Steve:

Why is it three Magi came from the "East," to anoint Jesus and verify his divinity (somewhat like how the Dalai Lamas are chosen), yet there was no Rabbi or priest from Judea or the close vicinities showing any interest or acknowledgement?

What happened when Jesus was a child, there are stories of him being in Egypt, Britain and quite recently, we heard credible evidence he was in India on a spiritual apprenticeship. Are any of these localities, and maybe others, part of where Jesus was schooled? The accepted narrative of Jesus is that he alone was unlike any other mortal and was chosen by the Creator to illuminate and guide. Is that correct or are there nuances lost in translation?

Equally, according to the accepted Biblical scholars and priests, it was Jesus only who is the revealer. However, in the Gnostic scriptures the case can be made, and has been by us, that Mary Magdalene and Jesus were partners in the revealing and teaching of wisdom. Which account and perspective is closer to the truth?

Mezreth:

There was no religion, only the acknowledgment of spirit. There have always been those who have seen spirit in their kin, but it has always been questioned through limited eyes. Culture wrapped around ritual, and then religion. When religion was born, it had the skeleton of agenda and the flesh of hierarchy.

Jesus was there and here and, in all places, all the time. There is no one. There were those who heard the universe's whispers and spoke to young ears. The others have not been honoured the same way as Jesus, for he was not the only one, nor was he the first. He earned his knowledge from another who has earned his knowledge from another, and to wake up to this knowledge and comprehend its gravity is a very rare thing.

Both are wrong, but there is one that is less wrong.

Steve:

That partnership chronicled throughout the Gnostic scriptures, isn't Platonic, not by a long shot. Jesus is described as the male who "kissed on the mouth often" his wife/consort Mary Magdalene. Often in texts the disciples ask Jesus "why do you love her more than us?" Yet in other biblical passages she is a prostitute, a woman of dubious morality, or at best a well-off financial backer; which version is correct?

In Gnostic scriptures, and in particular the Gospel of Thomas, Thomas is acknowledged as being the twin-brother of Jesus. Is that preface a metaphor or a genetic fact?

If so, is that an example of a brother following in his brother's footsteps in both going and staying in India?

Mary Magdalene was expelled from Judea and the destination was not of India or any other lands, but death at sea. The boat was without rudder, oars or sail, and none of over thirty volunteers who joined her on this journey were sailors. It was an understandable expectation none would survive. But upon nearing the shores of Gaul (France) Sarah, Jesus' and Mary's first-born daughter used her magic to lay down her coat or hair upon the water, which all walked across to solid ground and safety. The point being in that Gnostic account Jesus had a family and his daughter was also plying miracles, of which her father walked upon water, but his daughter widened and strengthened that same miracle in accommodating, not just one, but over thirty pairs of feet. Is this all true, and if so leads on to what some of Mary's feats?

Mezreth:

Jealousy twists the truth. Maybe today you will not be so blind to see the truth and speak it.

Children, parents and siblings, all of us, a family. The only difference is who chooses to see this truth determines where they are in the family.

There have been times when those who could see had to leave the land of the blind.

She, Sarah, was more of her mother's daughter than her father's.

Steve:

Mary converted all of southern Gaul to follow the teachings both Jesus and herself preached. She lived in a steep cave on the side of a mountain, sat in the cave naked, grew her hair long, was fed manna from Heaven by angels and waited for pilgrims to successfully climb up seeking wisdom, advice and her blessings. Isn't this exactly what some Gurus do in India?

Maintaining that geographical influence, in the Gnostic Scripture, Thunder the Perfect Mind, the female who wrote this is claimed to be either Isis, Eve or Mary Magdalene. The problem is the best Biblical scholars in the world are agreed its format has no parallel anywhere, except in a variety of ancient Indian Scriptures. Outside Mary actually being In India, neither Eve or Isis where even close, so once again I see this Indian link with both Mary and Jesus; is this a valid assumption?

In many Gnostic scriptures dealing with Jesus and Mary, there seems to exist a strong misogynist undercurrent in backroom and almost always it comes out of the mouth of Peter. More than once he openly threatens women, so much so that in the final verse in the Gospel of Thomas, Thomas was to close proceedings by highlighting the seminal split in morals and misogyny. "Let Mary leave us, for women are not worthy of life." Was this a fair reflection of the reason why Christianity broke into two camps/philosophies, the exoteric versus the esoteric?

Mezreth:

She heard the same teachings from the same source as the gurus. They all could listen. And so the universe spoke to them all.

The jungles were home to those who remember a time when Earth was a mere rock. The jungles grew from the dream of peace and the thickets became their walls. None were allowed to tread until a small group of runaways sought asylum. The Elementals were reluctant, but gave in to their pleas. However, they gave them warnings. The tiger will watch you if you obey our laws. This chance, this land transformed from a refuge to a piece of learning.

Words have more worth than conveying a thought. Words are secret powers of the universe. What is spoken, no matter how mundane, twist reality. Imagine the power of a few words. Because those words destroy everything.

Steve:

Speaking of esoteric there is a passage in the Gospel of Bartholomew where he questions Mary after Jesus and Mary returned to group after conducting some private ceremonies. Bartholomew asked Mary to share with him what they discussed and chanted. She declined warning him that if she did utter aloud such words the "fire would consume the world." That sounds a lot like alchemy and magic, was what Mary said possible?

After Jesus was crucified it is claimed he rose again three days after. Did that happen? Was a resurrection of flesh, or light from the soul? If it did happen what was its purpose?

In the Old Testament there is a prophecy of a final upheaval and then a thousand years of peace and harmony. What is your understanding and timing of that prediction.

Mezreth:

She knew the power of words and she knew their effect if they were heard by the wrong ears.

There is no life and death. There is only life.

Fear. The millennia of peace and prosperity for it is the herald of extinction. The golden age of man has always ended in fire greater than its father before. You must chase and fight for the golden age. This is true. But remember, your growth is hitched on the trials and challenges. The moment you are met with serenity, you will become soft and fall away into darkness. Remember what happened last time?

Transcript Fifteen
Chapter 26

Steve:

In the USA four objects were shot down recently, one is claimed to be a Chinese balloon, but as for the other three all we have are questions. General Van Herck, who is the head of the North American Aerospace Defence Command said that "they were calling them objects, not balloons, for a reason." However, then and until now they have refused to disclose what the reason is. Could Mezreth give us any clues as to what the reason is and why they will not reveal it to the public.

President Biden agreed that one object was "shaped like an octagon," another was the "size of small car" and third was a "cylindrical shaped object." He also conceded that none of the wreckage from these objects has been recovered, but having conceded they have no evidence went on to say the objects are "definitely not Chinese." How could he know this without examining the wreckage? Could you give us your explanation as to what these objects are and from where they came?

Just over three years ago a ceremony took place at Uluru. Was it successful, what actually happened and are those who really control this planet aware of this Event?

Mezreth:

They lie through the truth. You are being prepared for a new fear. A kind of fear that will overshadow the one for a mere disease.

There are factions even within the shadows. The lines have blurred and have broken, but they know they are being watched by you and us.

They know, and some even unwillingly participated. The tsunami crashed and now, the tides are reeling all into the sea.

Steve:

Was this ceremony part of the reason why you and so many other Alien races have taken such a long-term and intensive interest in Earthly affairs?

Dolores Cannon speaks of this planet ascension and likens it to two dimensions on offer and each person must choose which way to proceed. Is that a valid description?

She also used an analogy of two trains at a station and each person has to choose a train. As each day passes the distance between these trains gets greater. Have the trains left the platform?

Aunty Trudy Roberts told me that this year has been exceptionally sad, as so many of her relatives have died. She feels it has never been this bad, not just with her family but others, and puts this down to being part of the transformation process. Is she right?

It is her opinion this process of cleansing and change will continue for the next seven years leading up to 2030. I may be wrong but I feel it will be much earlier and countdown is not in years but months? Who is closer or is the line in the sand unknown?

I've seen my Elder Karno disappear, sing up eight hawks to circle above at the Standing Stones site, sing up eagles to accompany alongside us in a bus and heard stories from his wife of him instructing one of his apprentices to stand on top of a huge ant's nest for an hour and never get bitten because of the song he sang. Does every human on this planet have the latent capacity to do similar feats?

Mezreth:

No.

Its of the soul, not physicality.

You must remember that every passenger can leap out of a moving train at any time.

Phoenix.

It was, is and always will be.

All things that have consciousness affect consciousness.

Steve:

When humans are performing at this spiritual level, is this one of the reasons Aliens were drawn to this planet and to the humans, when we are functioning at their optimal mystical level?

You have said often since the Uluru ceremony that all the drama, chaos and injustice is a gift for each soul to embrace or contest, and it is designed to lead on to humans becoming part of a Cosmic community. If that happens, what can we offer the Aliens who have been a part of a community that spans the Universe and what can they offer or teach us?

Many of my friends, in particular one who will be watching this, are very much caught up in the unfairness and frustration caused by those running this crumbling show on Earth. They post and send out you tubes about this negativity, agonising over the wrongs and manipulation of the Cabal or moguls. This negative narrative has become a fundamental part of their life. Is this a healthy pursuit and what advice would you give them?

Mezreth:

Not quite. There have been species we have encountered that have shown greater potential, but we chose to close those dialogues. They became stunted and walled. We could not fill their cups without pouring out their egos. They could not learn, and we could not grow.

We want from you the same thing Akashi wants. How can one be all without all being one?

To quote 'if you stare into the abyss, the abyss stares back'. The pull is strong, its magnetic and lights a fire for justice, but it does not mean that one is immune to its effects of the downward spiral. You're here not only to protect and learn, but also to enjoy. Stop taking life so seriously.

Steve:

I wanted to leave this to be the last question, as I did ask you privately whether the three objects were from the Alien community and you said no they weren't, but added an intriguing comment as an aside, in stating that some of the Alien spaceship have been shot down using and adapting Alien technology. If that happened in America, China, Russia or quite a few other countries there would be like-for-like counter-measures. Was there any response towards those responsible? In them doing so doesn't that mean that the governments involved are fully aware of the presence of Alien craft and their benevolent intentions?

Mezreth:

'Those in charge,' 'those in power,' are utterly relative concepts. The truth is they may have great material and intellectual wealth, but they are slaves who think themselves as masters. They have been poor for generations. I don't speak for the other (E.T.) factions, but I know their voices whisper in their hungry ears. Those voices trust in the loyalty to greed. The powerful slaves are dying, there is no denying that, but the question we have is how many will allow them to be taken, too?

Transcript Sixteen
Chapter 27

Steve:

Ancient pyramids are spread throughout the world. Was this type of construction something humans invented, or was it given to us by Aliens?

Either way, who built them, and since to this time no-one has yet supplied a satisfactory answer as to how were they built?

What is their purpose? Mainstream academics assure us they are merely big coffins, while others insist it can generate enormous amounts of energy of some sort, or does it have some other function?

Do these pyramids still have the ability to work now? Is it an extinct relic of ancient days or waiting to be turned on again?

Mezreth:

It was introduced by the Zanashj, but human engineers and crafters adjusted the structure to fit this planet.

There are many ways to construct these structures, provided what the builder aims to do with it and what purpose they serve. Some were fitted to generate energy, others to process water, others to bridge communication grids and stabilise dynamic spatial sectors. To put simply, if the builder wants to enhance their own energetic pathways (of their own body,) they can construct a copper and/or crystalline pyramid frame with their bare hands before recharging and regenerating in the small alcove.

The Great Pylons of Old have been misunderstood since the Fall (Atlantean Cataclysm.) Many civilisations tried rebuilding their own versions in homage and worship due to their mystique. The Pylons were the key to an untold future of the ancient world. Their light had never been given the chance to brighten the world. A tragedy for those who understood their potential.

They were designed in a way to remove the need of current conventional power generating methods. The pylons are now active, but they are on standby. Their shape, mass, alignment, and the material perfectly curated for the place they were built on: an astral nexus point. It can be used again; you have an abundance of materials but lack the knowing.

Steve:

The pyramids and the Face on Mars, is that all random geological structures or made by Aliens, and if so, do they have some sort of connection/interrelationship with the pyramids on Earth? Was there a distant time when Mars could sustain life? And if so, what cataclysm was responsible for its destruction?

Are there any remaining bases/settlements on Mars, or when it comes to this, any other planet or moon in our solar system?

There is a lot of talk and rumours about a massive, buried pyramid that has been found in Alaska, and that the American scientists are trying to harness its energy? Is there any truth in this talk?

What is also been claimed is that the energy output of this pyramid could satisfy the power needs for all of Canada if they could control it. Is that true, and do they have the knowledge and capacity to actually work out how to control this pyramid?

Remaining in the same sophisticated technological vein. The story behind the Manhattan project conducted during WW2, is that a warship was transported somewhere and when it returned some sailors were melted into the steel and others were insane. What happened and why did it fail?

Mezreth:

Nothing about Mars was an accident, but it had become a tragedy. Mars was our kin's first choice to seed – it was a paradise until our genius was hijacked by pride.

We never left Mars., nor Saturn, nor her moons and Jupiter's.

Before biological life developed in this tiny golden twinkle, my kin had insisted on marking every star and world in their sights. Ask yourself, who were the ones who gave you this condition?

A single pylon cannot, but an operating cluster can. Many ancient structures have fallen into decay and ruin. Some are still active, but you need to be in our minds to know how to use them.

Phasing technology is one of the hallmarks of a civilisation ready for interstellar travel, but before that civilisation can join our interstellar community, they must be aware of the devastating dangers of it. If phasing is misused, nuclear contamination would be a dream of the past.

Steve:

Another huge stone construction that is still a mystery is Stone Henge in England. Is it also capable of generating energy, or a temple or does it serve some other purpose?

In regards to The Standing Stones site in Australia that we have examined in some detail, does it have the same powers/energy generation as Stone Henge? And inscribed on the rocks are symbols claimed to be First Language spoken on this planet; was that language, which is also called Soul Language, created by humans or given to us by Aliens?

I do know such monuments are not Mezreth's main concern and he is more interested in the progress or regression of individual souls. So, I wanted to close proceedings with two questions related to lives some souls are experiencing this time around.

What of those who have incarnated into bodies that are intellectually challenged; there are children I have taught with IQs too low to measure. They can barely talk and rarely if ever interact in a meaningful way with others. What do they gain or learn in a life so severely compromised?

Mezreth:

It was an attempt to build another type of pylon for unique tasks, but the builders lacked the precision, logistics and materials. Make no mistake, the engineers were descendants of Alkhemites and Atlanteans long after the Fall. They held the memory of those times but failed at recalling the wisdom.

The Standing Stones are older than the ruins of Stone Henge. Their power relied on the grounds they sat on, but their sequence and embedded ancient energy connected them to our Little Siblings. The First Language was made by man, but the first thought came from the stars.

They are blessed souls. Man sees them as beings imprisoned by their broken flesh, but their capacity for insight and meaning has reached heights that overshadow the 'healthy.' They are free of distractions, but their challenge is of an advanced kind – that has the power to accelerate themselves and all around them. Their weaknesses will shine a light on yours, as well as their strengths. Honour them, for they are greater teachers than myself.

Steve:

There is cult up here called Universal Medicine and their leader claims such people were evil in a past life and this is their punishment and they should be shunned and reviled. I personally find such talk repulsive. Could you share with us whether they are wrong and why holding such views is so troubling and dangerous to anyone thinking like that.

Mezreth:

Make no mistake, the karmic cycle is as tangible as your being. Remember, we all cycle through our actions and intentions – everything is attached with an opposite. If you wish to follow such doctrines, it's your own will – you may receive joy, companionship, wealth and prestige, but at the cost of the cycle crushing you. The Blessed Souls are your teachers disguised as the most vulnerable.

Transcript Seventeen
Chapter 28

Steve:

Are Yowies/Sasquatch/Yetis/etc. native and limited to this planet or are they a species found elsewhere. If they are only living on Earth how long have they been here?

While most people dismiss the talk of Yowies as being fictional, some do not and many who grant they may exist they see them as a sort of giant hairy ape of limited intelligence. Are they correct?

For those who feel Yowies are more aware and intelligent they often claim they can actually disappear before their eyes. Is that true and if so, how do they do something scientists would scoff at, and why do they feel the need to vanish?

Many people speak of the unique vocalisation of Yowies, and some even claim the actual noise has a multiple effect on the listener. We have sensed their noise can create a blanket of fear, and also forgetfulness. Is that down to our imagination (and others) or a cause and effect that is real?

Why is it they avoid and hide from humans?

Mezreth:

They are of earth and have always been, and wilfully always will be. Both of your kin came from One many millennia ago. You two are cousins, but one has been favoured by the Grandmother.

The wildmen ponder the same question about you.

They've walked the woods, deserts, and snow longer than you – they have met many curiosities about earth and learnt her secrets. They are aware of another that shares this world, but they became afraid and dug themselves deeper in their walls. And that fear that was once poisonous to them, has become a disease for all others on earth.

It's a blend of many things. The sound affects the atom, but the atom can affect itself. Remember how delicate one becomes when they are afraid; remember how dangerous they become.

They didn't want to be infected.

Steve:

Has this separation always been the case, was there a time in the past when they did not hide? And what happened to change this contact?

Why does their height vary from 2 meters to 5 metres?

Are Yowies the inspiration behind all the written accounts describing giants, or is that merely a different taller species of Hominid?

How long do Yowies live for?

Are they part of the reincarnation process on this planet, which would mean Yowies can incarnate into human bodies and also the reverse.

Where do they live? The issue being no-one looking for or researching Yowies has ever found a dwelling, lean-to or even a cave where they resided.

Mezreth:

You two were nearby for a long time – and once, you two were friends. However, one believed they were greater, productive, and more useful friend, and one day, that friend single-handedly changed the world without thinking about the other. Make no mistake, humans may have arrogance as their greatest sin, but the wildmen can hold grudges that outlast any stone.

Some groups simply need to be certain heights. Consider this: if humans are lions, then wildmen are tigers. Consider one's lone survival in the wilds of earth, would you need size and height, and strength on your side?

Oh, yes.

130 years in this realm, barring illness or injury or a broken heart.

Of course.

There are many hidden places on earth.

Steve:

Knowing that you told us earlier Yowies are even more antagonistic towards Aliens than humans, how is that fractured relationship travelling and is it a priority to resolve? And if so, why is it important?

It is our understanding, and that of Uncle Donny, that there are two types of Yowies-the physical hairy giants and the esoteric ephemeral beings that spend a lot of time in my bedroom and that of Evans.

Was it always two types of Yowies from the beginning, or did one evolve from the other, and if so, which type was first?

Do they understand human languages, and can they vocalise them if inclined?

Who are more intelligent, humans or Yowies?

In an earlier discussion you told us the quality you most admired in Yowies was their humility; could you elaborate further?

Mezreth:

Before there were wildmen and humans, there was one. Our children, who were misguided, sought to be gods of the stars. They came to earth and saw you, and wanted to change you. After some centuries, humans were born, while the wildmen were forced to retreat. Since then, when they see us in the skies, they believe it's the old, terrible times again.

The old ones eventually became blended with the curtain.

Of course, but if you pay attention, you can understand them.

Yes.

They know where they are, they know who they are, and they know their limitations. They have the power to find joy in moments and love in few. They see the world as home that welcomes them.

Of course, there will be another world that will offer the same challenges for the young. This is merely earth's turn.

Transcript Eighteen
Chapter 29

Steve:

Have you ever been sick? If so, what was this sickness and how often does it happen? If not, what procedure or microbe is responsible for your general eternal immunity?

Do Aliens who live on other planets experience sickness and disease?

Is there any other planet where those residing get as sick and have so many variations of ailments as those found on this planet?

Was there ever a time on this planet when people could self-heal and never got sick?

Why is there such a prevalence and variation in the types of sicknesses, and what purpose does this serve? Is it a punishment, retribution or just bad luck?

Why is it that the saying 'one man's meat is another man's poison' applies to all forms of curative medicines? A prescribed medicine may have no effect for some, for others a partial improvement and for others it works completely. During the last global epidemic everyone I know, bar myself, got sick. Why is there such a huge variation in symptoms and reactions?

Mezreth:

We don't have a body.

Of course, how else can one appreciate health and life?

Yes, and those who live on said worlds have become stronger because of it. Whereas others have seldom experienced equal trials to only succumb instantly upon first resistance.

Never.

If you seek a physical answer, then I can give you dozens. If you seek an esoteric answer, then I can give you hundreds. Without challenge, there is no life, my friend.

If every aura is distinguishable to a particular life form, then every cell is equally distinguishable. The biological standard is much thinner than you think, when we capped out medical knowledge, we were compelled to appreciate the complexity of life. No two were alike, in mind, body and soul. Even your kin don't fully understand the ocean's depths of the vessel you sail.

Steve:

Dolores Cannon has a somewhat radical take on what is a disease, and I would be interested in Mezreth's response. "Diseases are information. But if the body does not have the information from this disease, the body creates the demise. It is a very interesting format to think that actually a disease is an energy of importance, not an energy of negativity.'

Is Dolores Cannon (along with the statements of Original Old Way healers) right in her observation that "you're not supposed to ever be sick, never. The body is a miraculous machine that has been created to take care of itself and heal itself if we don't interfere." And if so, is she right in reminding humans that "every disease is the body talking to you."

Some apparently unfortunate souls are incarnated into a body that is born with life-long afflictions that just can't be self-repaired either through the bodies' defence mechanisms or any form of conventional medications. Why does this happen, and what is the best recovery program?

A question from my wife of a somewhat lighter nature that relates to her Aunty who was born with a port wine stain birth mark on her face. Is this just a random event or does it carry substance due to previous lives and decisions?

This constant sickness and spreading of disease, was this a natural device created by Nature to cull and control population, or an external manifestation of the inner turmoil and fearfulness simmering within each person?

Mezreth:

All matter contains data, but the key is how the reader decodes it.

That statement is technically correct, but its pregnant with misconceptions.

Is it for them to heal or for others to heal?

Its possible for the scarred soul to scar its new vessel.

Disease is part of life, if you constantly fight against it, you will always lose. Embrace~

Steve:

In giving a perspective to this general sickness is the reality that the soul is eternal, and each incarnation is merely a second on clock of life which will pass. But what of a baby born with severe disabilities leading on to a premature death. What was gained during this brief painful cameo and what was the purpose served in leading such short traumatic life? Why did they agree to incarnate, and for whose benefit?

What advice would you offer to the many who are seriously ill and are tempted to give in to the despair and bodily disrepair?

Will the oncoming earthly transformation have any impact on the continued existence of these diseases and ailments?

Mezreth:

There are many things that occur beyond our understand, but we believe their purpose was to serve themselves and others.

Though the soul is immortal and has experienced many lives, each life is unique. Embrace these precious moments for they will never be repeated.

No, but there will be a different outlook on how ailments affect you. To me, you are all fortunate.

Transcript Nineteen
Chapter 30

Steve:

How was Atlantis destroyed, what mechanism or action was responsible?

Was everyone in Atlantis killed in the crystals exploding, or did some residents escape or were elsewhere when that location was destroyed?

The Younger Dryas marks out a major rapid global cataclysm where, according to the archaeologists, 80-95% of the human population was wiped out. Was that due to Atlantis exploding or a different event?

The many pyramids and civilisation of ancient Egypt, was that an attempt to revive the structures and ethics of Atlantis yet again?

Was it a straight copy or were amendments and additions included?

Mezreth:

The crystals stopped Atlantia's breath, but Atlantia was dead long before.

The few who were away survived, they mourned by attempting to reclaim their former glory. They never could.

The Atlantean Cataclysm was sparked when the island died, but the survivors rode the waves of destruction for centuries – leading deaths of communities, cities, and whole cultures into the After.

The Plateau was a representation of human ingenuity, brilliance, and moral cooperation. Every human of every background had their lives immortalised in those stones. The Plateau was what the Atlanteans wanted for the future – but the bricks crumbled all the same with their morals.

Yes. Many cultures contributed their own desires on these machines, long after Atlanteans became a memory.

Steve:

Those pyramids how were they constructed, we are told by present day experts tens of thousands of labourers spent decades hauling massive stone blocks up wooden ramps measuring kilometres using copper blades to shape the stone. Is that correct, or was the technology far more advanced?

When, why, and how did the Egyptian civilisation begin to fail like its predecessor?

The Greeks claimed the Egyptians knew all about Atlantis and in particular their demise, if so, why was it they seemed to repeat the same mistakes?

My interest is in the physical aspects of Egyptian gods that almost invariably have animal features and totems, which is very much an Australian Original tradition. Was Australia the source for this human/animal depiction?

Are we right in our constant assertion that ancient Egyptians came to Australia thousands of years ago?

Mezreth:

When the Plateau was merely land, hundreds of minds came together to advance their understanding of reality – to push the limits of knowledge. They almost succeeded. They had to invent things specially for the project. Many scientists, scholars, engineers, and priests had their lives dominated by their obsessive wants to make their mark. They wanted to witness the wonders of the universe act before them – in service to them, but they failed and now, all of them had been forgotten by their descendants.

Egypt was home for many civilisations over the millennia, all had unique languages, philosophies, and ways of seeing. However, they had all succumb to greed and lust for power. Despite their great ability to ward off Atlantean survivors, they eventually became the new richest nation in the world – and yet again, they had been tainted by the same old thing.

Because they believed they were uncorrupted and eventually believed they were incorruptible – that was always the start.

Australia was the source of inspiration for all human cultures.

The ancient Alkhemites knew about the Lemurians for many millennia, but they had especially known the strained relationship between Atlanteans and Lemurians. The Alkhemites sought to resurrect that old friendship, and so they had – for a time.

Steve:

If so, were they seeking spiritual guidance, wisdom and magical knowledge or knowledge of advanced Australian technology?

Why were, according to Lea, the Atlanteans banished from Lemuria/Australia?

We have spoken often about the three rings from Atlantis and that they had a powerful role in the destruction of Atlantis. What went wrong and why were two buried in Australia at Hill End (33 degrees south of Equator) and the third in Scotland?

The rings began with best of intentions then everything went wrong, what was the fundamental flaw in the path these rings took?

In regards to the two rings recovered at Hill End, was permission gained from the local Original tribe in burying them and why was Australia chosen?

According to Aunty Beve and Frederic Slater the Egyptians learnt about hieroglyphic pictograph from Original Australians who had already invented this style of written communication. Are they correct?

Mezreth:

The ancient world knew about the first men's story, but some wanted to understand it.

The Lemurians saw a shadow behind the Atlanteans. It had dawned on them that these people were on a clock and that their sun will be setting soon, forever.

They went to places that most of the ancient world was afraid to tread.

The rings had no choice in what their fates had become. Their masters and keepers had gifted them to the worst people, allowing their magic to enhance and unbury their darkest natures of their new holders' souls. Over and over. Enhance, destroy, absorb – grow. Enhance, destroy, absorb – grow. Their makers invented an incurable disease.

Those rings were ripped from dead hands, and once it was realised what they truly were, they were given to those that would never use it and had the power to willingly forget that power.

Art, language and thought came from Lemuria.

Steve:

A question from Jeffrey relates to whether Egyptians and Atlanteans are contemporary in existing at the same time, or were Atlanteans a far more ancient race?

Just to confirm the geography and locality of Lemuria, was ancient Australia (Sahul) part of Lemuria and are the Old Way Original Elders the true custodians of the Lemurian legacy?

Although not quite on topic, something about the Schuman resonance needs to be raised asap, so it has to sneak in. Yes, often the measurements often run off the page, but an unbelievable extension has just taken place that has caused a great deal of discussion. I've seen the read out showing a completely different energy form that looks so much like exactly how our human DNA is depicted. Is this the beginning of the final stage, is the planet now reaching into our DNA to either prepare us if we are able to absorb or refuse entry as some of us just are not ready to transform?

Mezreth:

Atlanteans uplifted many cultures that became formidable nations over the millennia. Alkhem was one of them, however, the people who called their once-jungles home had been there far longer than their sister-country across the water.

Lemuria never lived without the wand and her wielders.

Beginnings and ends happen within every beat.

Transcript Twenty
Chapter 31

Steve:

There are two theories in regard to the settlement of humans in Australia. One insists that around 50-60,000 years ago a few Africans sailed accidentally to Australia and once there never left, and until the British invasion they remained isolated. Our theory compiled in consultation with Original Elders, is that the Original humans were always here. Which take on the ancient past is correct?

My genetic Denisovan content is 4.7%, why is it that only Australian Original people have a Denisovan reading of above 2.5%? As it is agreed that Denisovans never went to Australia, and we are told that the Africans once coming here never left, so this reading creates a real issue. Can you explain how and when this contact occurred?

Was Australia ever part of Lemuria, and if so, when and how did Lemuria disappear or sink?

Mezreth:

There is only one first man. And the first men have always been here.

Gardeners throw seeds on rich soils. Which ones will become flowers, which will become vines, and which will become trees – but most never take at all. There's no certainty; only hope. Sometimes a child wanders into the garden. Takes a seedling to look at it, then they play with it. Sometimes they mix a seedling with another or even one from their own garden. The child re-plants the new seedling on a fresh plot, continuing to play and taunt it until they get bored…or discover their new plaything has grown thorns and others had grown venoms. The child didn't expect this, nor did the gardener. By all reason it was a mistake, but how fortuitous for the seedling that it grew exactly what was needed. The child and gardener then realise they were never in charge at all.

Lemuria was here before us and will always be.

Steve:

There are Creation Stories in Australia, one talks about the Seven Sisters from the Pleiades where they came to Australia. Did that actually happen and what impact did they have on the Original people?

Slater's interpretation of the rock engravings at Burragurra is about beings coming to this planet from across the Milky Way. It goes on to add that the first human males were actually buried in the ground for some time and re-emerged when nature was in full bloom. Is that correct? And equally it makes it clear females were with them, but does not state that they were buried, that could be that because it is male story it is not mentioned but also happened, or maybe they were not buried. What is your take on the females' role in the beginning?

Bruce Pascoe has been heavily criticised for claiming that Original people did farm the land using a form of no-dig agriculture, where seeds were scattered on the ground or in ashes or soil where compost/scraps were deposited. Is that correct?

Following down the same 'rabbit-hole' we believe that there was a time way back when Original people did use highly advanced technology. Is that correct, and if so, when and why did they abandon this practise?

Why were two Atlantean rings buried at the same place in Australia?

Mezreth:

There was a time when our little siblings became the parents we had failed to be. They confronted us afterwards, saying if we wanted to do this, then there are a million ways to do it wrong, but only one to do it the proper way. Since then, we tried to honour that.

What was first and what was last?

The first men had accomplished many firsts.

They stopped just before their ears deafened to Lemuria's warning song.

So only the grandmother can take that burden.

Steve:

Now with a general setting established we wanted to look at Old Way practises, in particular the skills some would claim to be magical. I saw Karno disappear and call up and talk to eagles; was this the norm way back and is it, as Karno insisted, a talent we still could access?

It is one thing to communicate with animals, but insects are a leap further. Karno's wife Christine told me of a time he took Wirritjin down to an ant's nest, that only days before he placed a goanna carcass on and was devoured within an hour. After breaking into song accompanied by clapsticks, he told Wirritjin to stand on the same ant's nest, over close to an hour and he kept singing and not once was Wirritjin bitten. How could this happen?

Why is it all Original people have totems, normally animals but also can include shells and vegetation, in Karno's case it was the wedge-tailed eagle. Does that mean under the right conditions we could communicate with our totem?

In Original society having a series of initiation ceremony was an integral part of life and death. What purposes does initiation serve and do some or all Alien societies have some form of initiation? If so, could you give some examples as to what they did?

Mezreth:

Of course. Can't you hear the music?

He heard the melody and played along.

Not just that.

Life is a privilege few souls get to experience. Because of this, life is not for meandering. Every stage must be earnt and should be honoured. The Xanik-Fan burrow themselves deep into the cities, but for all children to be grown, they dance with the sands for days. The Ezoni infant is first taught how to listen and play music before they utter their first word so they can sing to the shivering forests.

Transcript Twenty-one
Chapter 32

Steve:

Dolores Cannon is adamant that "ETs are living now on the Earth, they are everywhere among your friends, neighbours and even relatives. Their blood flows through our veins, we are as much brothers and sisters to beings from the stars as we are to the animals of the Earth." What is fascinating is that Dolores makes no distinction between Mezreth, us and all types of animals, is she correct? Does that mean we have all incarnated into different animal forms in previous lives?

Dolores extends not only the participants but localities in claiming "through reincarnation we come and go to different locations, earth is merely a school." Does that mean nearly all, if not all, present-day human residents have incarnated in other constellations? And is this school, which you have often said it is one of the most difficult schools in the Cosmos to learn from, have the most taxing subjects in this Earthly curriculum?

Mezreth:

Soul has no species, race or sex. Soul is soul. You would be surprised at what runs in our veins if you look a little deeper.

All life is a school. Life will test your buoyancy in water – no matter what, but if you wish to prove you are a strong swimmer, go where you may drown.

Steve:

While deposited in the realm of difficult challenges, our religious beliefs are such a tortuous path to travel. We have religions and sects/cults who believe their teachings exclusively guarantee admission to 'heaven'; others if instructed by their leader will commit suicide or mass genocide of unbelievers and believe such atrocities will gain God's approval and endorsement. The many inquisitions sanctioned every type of torture and depravity but was done so firmly convinced it was approved by God. They carried out warfare slaughtering women and children, and even after doing the most heinous acts of depravity genuinely believe if they confess and feign contrition God will forgive any indiscretion, and so it continues. Do other Alien civilisations match this diversity in beliefs in relation to what the Creator will approve, or are their understandings of life, death and ascension more consistent, compassionate and uniform?

We want to pursue a topic raised in our previous Q and A in relation to animals and our relationship with them. At the supposed top end of the 'soul-pecking order,' what is the difference between the soul of a dolphin and human?

Trees do communicate, but do they also have an independent soul or spirit?

But what about ants and bees, is their soul a collective unit, do they think and exist collectively? Is one ant similar to one flake of skin on our body?

Mezreth:

Every act or inaction serves the next life you will lead. Most doctrines make this very clear, but it's rarely practiced. Just as rare as love. Humans can create any excuse to slaughter each other, and using religion is a civilised excuse to behave like the devil. Make no mistake, my friend, many species have this monster inside them. The Raivan would set their families and clans ablaze if they were forbidden from practising their beliefs, the Xannians used to throw their outdated elderly in deep sand holes and let the sun pull every drop of water from their bodies. And the Zanashj recrafted the flesh of heretics into fine chairs, tables, and other upholstery. When love and hate meet in battle, it turns us all into savages.

None.

All life has soul.

Every speck floats in the sea of consciousness. It varies in depth. However, to deny one thing possesses consciousness, makes you indeed quite shallow.

Steve:

Scientists assure us that even though we use no more than 15% of our brain and that this is the norm. Is that really the case? And has it always been like this?

How much more could we access and what capacities lay dormant inside the unused section of the brain?

Do all other animals use so little of their brain or is it running at full capacity?

Is that lack of engagement with so much of the largest organ in our body the fundamental block to our ascension? Is that always meant to be so, and will it continue like this after the planet transforms and ascends?

Let's talk about dogs, I have heard often the recent claims that dogs have taken on a new role in showing humans the path to unconditional love. Is that a valid observation?

Recently my wife keeps showing me videos of dogs doing things that require the highest order of thinking, way above what scientists assume they are capable of; is that because they are now living with us and are getting smarter?

And when it comes to getting smarter, human's recent track record of reality TV viewing habits and blind unquestioning obedience and acceptance, questions whether our intelligence is declining. Is this a recent descent or has it been par for the course for some time?

Mezreth:

The brain is a tool that can be extended with the right guidance. There was a time when you could do far more than what you can do now, but these current limitations are a secret blessing – are they not?

You already have the power to do it all, you just lack the training.

Theirs is greater than yours.

The block of your ascension is your wilful ignorance. No path has ever been impossible to travel with humility. There is no shame admitting to not knowing or being wrong, that is the key for prosperity.

No.

It's the other way around.

Excessiveness leads to indecisiveness, and indecisiveness leads to apathy, and apathy leads to laziness. If you truly want to be more intelligent, ask more; speak less, want less so you may value more.

Questions from our Subscribers
Subscriber 1:

I was asked to raise the issue of Artificial intelligence and your opinion of AI. I want to add a setting to his question because I know AI is used by many Alien groups and that one portrait Lea drew in the first Interview book is AI creation, so clearly it does work, but right now on this planet amongst all the chaos and greed, I think what the subscriber was thinking is that right here it is just too risky. So the question is right now with our present leaders and fearful lives, what it comes down to is a choice of allowing AI to just flourish and spread or stop it now and go no further. Which path would you advise?

Subscriber 2:

A gentleman who we have been in contact for some who does have an extensive knowledge of many aspects of the real histories asked me to ask Mezreth about his contention that in Australia long ago this continent was used, as it was in early British times after the invasion, as a penal/prisoner colony and the ones imprisoned were really not good people. He claims that the ancient Original tribes were deceived and tricked into believing that they were Egyptian. I know many others have been here for so long, but never of a much earlier prisoner colony. Is he correct?

Mezreth:

The Arinu have A.I.s running their government. There is no corruption or energy theft. They are left to pursue greater personal ambitions without worrying about leeches growing fat. You can co-exist and thrive with A.I., but you do not have the current maturity or speed to handle something like this. You can barely wrangle the internet. Unfortunately, we know what memes are.

The first men had met many more civilisations than the European kingdoms ever had combined. They are the first, they are the oldest, and they knew who and what was over hundreds of millennia. However, over these immense timespans, it's not impossible for one group to mistake another. Mistakes do occur, but knowing the vigilance of history the first men have, it is unlikely that it was a trick.

Subscriber 3:

Regarding the changing of timelines due to us not being ready, who can make a decision on the earth's ascension slowing down, how is that even possible? Wasn't the transition all related to the earth ascending?

The conferences are very geared toward bringing back old way teachings. Where and how do we learn these ways?

What's this work about bringing ceremony to those in Alice Springs and how can we get involved in that?

Subscriber 4:

Did the explosion of Atlantis cause the Younger Dryas? (Sea level rise/ the Holecene)?

Did this then cause 'The Flood' and change the world map?

Was Atlantis in the Atlantic Ocean?

Is that why it's called the Atlantic?

Was Atlantis an empire not a continent?

Mezreth:

Ascension is as slow as the ticking of a clock. It is happening, always, everywhere and all the time, but the speed of this invisible clock is beholden to the ones living within its lines. You could have ascended at the end of 2020, you could have ascended a century ago, you could have ascended 20,000 years ago. It didn't happen because you knew in your heart that you weren't ready. And who wants to live in a half-world?

Speak less; listen more.

~

No, the Younger Dryas was caused because of the death of the Atlantean Empire. The destruction of the Atlantic Island was not the trigger, but the lack of knowledge and equipment in its wake allowed the Younger Dryas to occur.

Atlantia's destruction was not the cause of the flooding, but its absence abated it.

Its ghost is still there.

Yes.

The Atlantean Empire is dead, but it still haunts earth.

Subscriber 4:

Did the Atlantis explosion cause the Sahara Desert at Alkheim (Egypt?

Mezreth:

No, that was after a war and a natural disaster – some say it's the same thing.

Transcript Twenty-two
Chapter 33

Steve:

Mainstream history has a narrative that maintains that dinosaurs became extinct 65,000,000 million years ago, then there was a huge gap until hominids began roaming across the planet less than 10,000,000 years ago with modern humans turning up less than half a million years ago. To begin with they were very crude and limited in technology until about six thousand years ago. How close to the truth and timing is this interpretation of our existence on this planet?

When did humans first appear on this planet?

According to the Original Seven Sister's Dreaming story, Slater's research and our research we are of Alien genes and ancestry, is this correct?

It is claimed that in much earlier times were humans all living in caves, or could it be there were earlier advanced civilisations?

Mezreth:

The merit of sophistication is not technology, it's awareness. Earth's history is far richer and deeper than the bones it has left behind. Constructing a story, no matter how thorough you analyse and uncover every buried piece, is still only a story. You may know how these great creatures walked, what they ate, but have you ever asked what they thought? Did they have language? Did they have their own elders? Did they have a culture and laws they abided by? What did they see when they saw their own reflections in the mirrored waters? What did they feel when the sun's warmth touches their backs or when the stars winked back at them? Do you ask who they were instead of what they were? We miss them.

There are many answers to this popular question, not one of them is true and yet, all are correct. Consider this one of many answers: it will take another several hundred millennia for a human to walk on this freshly formed world.

Parts of you are.

Humans walked to cities from caves, then from cities back to caves. On and on this cycle continued and will continue for a few more times.

Steve:

In those much more ancient times, were there times when humans travelled into space towards distant constellations?

Of course, that leads on to the multiplicity of accounts relating to Lemuria and Atlantis, when did that begin and end?

During those times, was the technology, lifestyle and understandings superior or inferior to how things are today?

What is depressing about the accounts of the most recent history beginning about 6,000 years ago is the consistency of never-ending series of wars and conflicts, it paints a picture that suggests that warfare and aggression is merely an essential part of human nature and the natural state of human affairs. Is this true, have we always been at loggerheads with each other?

Both ourselves and Slater believe there was once one global language we all spoke, and as it is in the Bible, when the Tower of Babel fell, we began to speak different tongues, and this event and misfortune was a seminal cause of our fall from grace. Is that a reasonable historical observation?

Mezreth:

Humans too walked from this world, back and forth, but there will come a time when humans walk away from earth for the last time.

Lemuria was the first and one of the few remaining ancient civilisations, unlike Atlantia and the many societies that have come and gone throughout memory. Lemuria will still be here until the last cell dies.

Superiority and inferiority are concepts we have discarded in ages past. They strip nuance from the lived experience. Today, you do not live better or worse than those who had been before you, but there is a deprivation of spirit. And in history, spirit's absence has been an omen before a great fall.

Of course. However, aggression is not a thing to be exorcised or abhor. It's a part of you, as much as love is. You must manage your demons and angels, because if one were to dominate the other, then it will always be you who suffers.

No. Diversity in words means a diversity in language, and therefore, a diversity of thought.

Steve:

Is both Slater's and Karno's written account of the First Language correct, and if so, would it be a good idea to resurrect and record this language? If this is recommended, how would it help?

Moving off-world to our neighbouring planet Mars, was there ever a time when Mars supported life and if so, was it merely amoebas and germs or something far more complex?

If there was life on Mars was that a natural event or introduced from elsewhere?

What brought this time of life on Mars to a close?

Will there ever be a time in the future when either us or Aliens from above could resettle Mars?

Mezreth:

You need to know where you come from before you can take another step forward.

Mars was long before earth. Mars was our first choice, but through our choices, earth became our only option.

Mostly introduced.

We did.

We never left Mars.

Transcript Twenty-three
Chapter 34

Steve:

When were the glyphs at Kariong first engraved?

Why was it decided to engrave and why this location?

What does it say?

People claim it was chiselled, but there are so many curves and circles that are continuous and lack any straight lines, what tools were used?

There seems to be clearly more than one style of writing, some glyphs are smaller, others shallower, one set is two hundred metres away. By our count we can see at least three different scribes. Is that correct?

Aunty Beve claims the upper passage is Egyptian but all the other two walls are written much earlier and some of it was written by Original people. She went on to claim the ancient Egyptians came here to learn earth magic, culture and hieroglyphs. Is she right?

If so, what first drew the Egyptians to Australia and when did they start sailing here?

Mezreth:

In the twilight days of the first tongue.

That place is grander and deeper than what is said. The signs aren't the magic, they merely point to it.

Of who was and will be, how many times it will happen and when time rolls into nothingness. It speaks about an era and people who had arrived there for the first time, only to realise they were there many times before.

A thing as delicate as a pen, but harder than steel. The first women know.

They were added by the same people who returned over many eras.

They were far the first who came to learn from the first men, but they were one of the last.

When the Atlanteans were blinded, the others seized an opportunity to save themselves from them.

Steve:

There is film of a white serpent coming out of the walls. Nearly every photo of the Grandmother Tree captures a huge array of colours radiating outwards. What causes this?

Apart from Egypt, did other ancient civilisations come to Australia? If so, why?

What comment can you offer to an Original spokesperson who said the tree is nothing special and is merely a tourist device?

If it is indeed a sacred tree and site, was it made sacred by humans or the earth?

Is this all history and merely a relic of the past, or is this site still functioning?

Developers want to build and subdivide on a star platform of massive proportions and claim as long as the actual site is not damaged everything nearby is open slather. However, Old Way spirituality of sacred sites insists all sites are interconnected through ley lines and to cut through or damage the connected lines of energy damages the entire grid. Are they right?

There is a star map above, clearly made through the application of an Original stick, stone and bones tool kit, it has been dated at 4,600 years by Sydney University. Why was it made and what does it commemorate?

Mezreth:

For every one thing you see there, there are a thousand things you don't.

Everyone knew about Lemuria.

There are mouths where ears should be.

Lemuria.

Can you turn off a crystal?

The tragedy is any changes to all land and water affect nexus points. However, considering that they are dwindling in number and power, this site is not one you can afford to lose. Unless you wish to delay your progression again.

A celestial remembrance that cycles the right time.

Steve:

Because I previously asked about whether you knew Aunty Beve, and you responded in the positive, could you give a character reference for Aunty Beve?

Aunty Beve gave a group of us ceremony at the Grandmother Tree not long before she passed and she sang the song of "the Four Winds"; what did all of this ceremony do to the site and those who were invited?

Since she has passed have you had any further contact with her, and if so, is she still concerned and involved in the struggle to save this land?

On a completely different topic, before and after the transitional ceremony conducted at Uluru on December 2020 we kept telling people very soon after the Earth would ascend and each person would be assessed as to whether they had earnt the right to remain. We spoke of a timeframe that never reached one decade. But it is now more like a century. Why has the timing been so dramatically extended and could you give us a feel as to how this time will pass on Earth?

Mezreth:

She is a Lemurian soul, she was born with knowledge, but it took much of her life to understand it.

To give you a friendship with the nexus.

No one is afraid here, but all are involved there.

Change comes every day, but it will take a million right changes to reach the ending you wish. However, don't assume it will be an age free of wrongs.

Transcript Twenty-four
Chapter 36

Steve:

In our last presentation we focussed on the Kariong site with particular reference to engraved hieroglyphs, the sacred Grandmother Tree, the construction and destruction sanctioned by those in control and plans to rezone and subdivide. You have told us more than once if this site was destroyed there would be negative consequences not just there but throughout the planet. Could you be more specific in what they are and how an actual archaeological site has the capacity to react at such a level.

You recently asked a lady we know to return to this site and perform some ceremonies. Was this successful and what actually happened?

One of the workers was badly injured and this led to a Westpac helicopter transporting this person to a hospital in Sydney. Was this an accident or was this a consequence of being part of the damage and explosions?

Mezreth:

If one brick shatters, it collapses the archway, and then eventually the building will fall in. There are a hundred things you see, but ten thousand that you cannot. It's not your place to know what every one of those things are, you already know its value and will do everything you can to protect it from you own.

To slow the cracking bricks.

Those who live on that land know the faces of their visitors, but more importantly, they know every heart. What punishment you saw dealt may have been a direct result of the site's destruction, but there are many unseen steps leading to that moment. The wheel of give and take is ever-moving, what good that visitor has done and the bad has been weighed and acted upon. What happened to them was a demonstration of this wheel moving, but what about the other visitors who were there? What about the ones who had desecrated the rocks and trees during and long before the site's cremation? Yes, the one's who live on that land did respond to the destruction and seemingly spared the others, but remember, there are many things that don't appear plainly, their wheels are turning – even now.

Steve:

The 300 odd hieroglyphs engraved into the sandstone walls have led on to many interpretations, some claim it is merely graffiti and others insist it is a message from ancient Egyptians or the Gods. Can you give us your understanding as to what the content of this engravings means.

The Grandmother Tree is certainly an enigma. On so many occasions people take photos of the tree, and it always has a variety of colours radiating out from the tree. What is going on here, surely it cannot be due to so many different cameras malfunctioning, what is coming out of this sacred tree, and why?

The Women's Table, so many women have laid on this curved clearly artificial formation and each has a reaction that is unique to them alone. What is going on here, and where or what is its energy source?

The Men's Circle does not create the same dramatic reaction, but it still works on what seems to be a more subtle level. What are the dynamics of this site?

Karno told me often that if someone claims a site is sacred but has no link to "as on top," it is not legitimate. He was adamant all sacred sites must have a connection to somewhere out there is space. Is he correct, and if so, why is this a mandatory requirement?

There is so much archaeology in Australia that has an ancient Egyptian imprint, why did they come here, what were they seeking?

Mezreth:

That place is older than my name. A thousand hands graced the engravings over the millennia, there were those who wrote the original tale, then some came later to add their own truths to it – then there were those who came to reward their delusions on the stone. Every stone speaks of a different age.

They say that cameras can see what the eye cannot, but that isn't true. You already know the tree is singular, or more accurately put, you know it is not a tree.

The same place where all artifacts and sites gather their power from.

Like all sites, it is to encourage and stir something deep within the visitor.

Of course, every site reflects one on another world.

The first men know.

Steve:

We have seen archaeology from other locations, but we do suspect that not all other visitors did come here for the same reasons as the Egyptians. Could you give a brief summary as to why Phoenicians, the Chinese, Spanish and Portuguese sailed to Australia, and did they get what they came for?

Mezreth:

You already know.

Transcript Twenty-five
Chapter 38

Steve:

There are two written versions of Jesus' life and actions, one is recorded in the Bible nearly everyone is familiar with, and another strand referred to as Gnosticism was hidden and often destroyed. Which account is closer to what actually happened during his ministry?

If they both contain mistakes or inconsistencies, what are they?

In both the Gnostic accounts of the Gospel of Thomas and Thomas the Contender, Jesus makes constant reference to Thomas being his brother, and moreover, his twin brother. Is Thomas his brother, and does this extend into being his twin brother?

The notion of twelve disciples may have two levels to consider. First up why is the number twelve so important?

In the Gnostic scripture Pistis Sophia it mentions nineteen disciples of which seven were women, while traditional Biblical accounts do concede there were women, but refers to them as "followers,." Which is deliberately a lesser term. Which account is closer to the truth?

Mezreth:

Truths are hidden; lies are displayed.

Many, however, the greatest of these errors are the few events that had happened, were not experienced by the supposed names in the books.

He was blood of few and brother to many.

It represents the aspects of a soul's nature, thereby, representing the many faces of Akashi (universe and it's dimensions.)

In truth, all were followers because they were students, but those few were considered less than their fellows.

Steve:

We recently had a highly respected Indian scholar who went into great detail in describing a time when Jesus and Mary were in India, as was the case with Thomas very soon after the crucifixion. But were they there first then moved on to the Middle East, or was this more a matter of the same type of duet/archetypes existing in different places at the same time?

Clearly the content of the Gnostic scripture Pistis Sophia is very challenging to all mainstream versions simply because when the resurrected Jesus invited his disciples to ask any question they wish, close to ninety percent of the questions asked came from Mary Magdalene. In fact, in one section, she asks 26 questions in a row. Why is it her role is so dominant?

In the Dialogue of the Saviour Mary makes a statement where it would seem she is revealing truths to Jesus he does not know, when declaring she wishes to take Jesus away from the disciples to instruct Jesus in "the mystery of the truth." In the Gospel of Thomas, she asks Jesus "what are your followers like?" In the Gospel of Philip, the disciples ask Jesus why do "you kiss Mary on the mouth often" and why do "you love her more than us?" We have Mary as the one he loves the most, revealing wisdom to Jesus he is lacking and clearly separating herself from his disciples. This leads on to the crucial question in this partnership, who is principal revealer, Mary or Jesus?

Mezreth:

Finally.

The teacher must challenge the student.

He paid for her wisdom with his name.

Steve:

During the compilation of the traditional Bible all gnostic texts and scriptures were deemed unworthy, Thomas was rejected primarily because no mention of miracles was made, it is 114 sayings or responses to questions made by Jesus, why was it the mention of miracles was chosen to be the hallmark of what was included in chronicling Jesus' life and ministry?

The same supernatural topic of miracles is equally dominant in the Old Testament, but is this mystical obsession due to earlier events from the local area or was it part of a very ancient Dreaming narrative that originated in Australia?

In both the Gospel of Thomas and Gospel of Mary, Peter is clearly openly antagonistic towards Mary insisting that "all women are unworthy of breath" and also called her a liar. Is this merely a reflection of the rampant misogyny that was a part of the times, or does this animosity run deeper?

Did Mary and Jesus have children?

The three Mary's (Magdalene, Mother Mary and her sister Mary Salome) were the ones who first saw that the crypt Jesus was interred within was open and the stone boulder that acted as a door had rolled away. What is worthy of reflection is that it states they met Jesus in his resurrected form, but they first thought this ascended being was the "gardener." If Mary Magdalene was his wife, along with his mother and aunty in attendance, surely they would have immediately recognised him. That being an undeniable truth why did they use the term gardener? Does it have a much deeper meaning?

Mezreth:

Do not be weary of worshipping any idols, be weary of the idol-makers.

All things are conceived in the Dream.

Forgive them, for they know not what they do.

Many.

No matter how far apart in age or in distance, all our children refer to us as gardeners. They have never been closer to understanding the truth.

Blended Answers

Here are most of the separate responses given in the transcripts which have been sorted and categorised into twelve categories. We occasionally provided a few words or sometimes a bit more, solely to set out clearer links as to how this passage relates to the heading chosen.

1. Life Choices and Challenges
Humans create innovative ways to cheat the test.

Make no mistake, the karmic cycle is as tangible as your being. Remember, we all cycle through our actions and intentions-everything is attached with an opposite. If you wish to follow doctrines with absolutes, it's your own will-you may receive joy, companionship, wealth and prestige, but at the cost of the cycle crushing you. The blessed souls are your teachers disguised as the most vulnerable.

This is Mezreth's answer to my raising the issue of those who carry huge handicaps through birth.

They are the blessed souls. Man sees them as beings imprisoned by their broken flesh, but their capacity for insight and meaning has reached heights that overshadow the 'healthy.' They are free of distractions, but their challenge is of an advanced kind-that has the power to accelerate themselves and all around them. Their weaknesses will shine a light on yours, as well as their strengths. Honour them, for they are greater teachers than myself.

We are flawed because there would be no reason to continue this. This is an essential part of spiritual development, because you have to identify the wrongs before you can identify the rights. Unfortunately, on Earth, we do have this predilection for self-loathing and so people tend to listen more to self-criticism over self-love first. Self-love is a vehicle to salvation, but not many understand what self-love truly means. So, I speak in ways that express clearer parts of this idea for you: you self-hate when you succumb to lounging an hour longer than you want, you self-hate when you tell yourself you are higher and more religious than all others. You must resist these small beliefs. Self-love is doing anything you can to live, not survive, even if it takes you to places of pain.

The human condition is not exclusive to humans. No one will ever be free of it. The difference is we devoted more time to communication and understanding of each individual, what their strengths and weaknesses are. We know why someone is the way they are. We know why they have made their choices. And we try to facilitate environments where they flourish. They are like seeds, but no two seeds are alike.

Upon death, an explosion of consciousness happens. It pours into everything. And everyone who is around the deceased, partially embeds itself into the relative material world around it, but the surviving soul, it departs if it chooses to do so. Some choose to linger and bond with their old world. Some are lost and others wander.

When souls depart life, they shed parts of the former personality, but what they were in life was returned to something more balanced. Some souls wish to wait. What some souls wish is to find other fields. But if there is a strong bond to the living, then they often stay.

If you want to master content, you will. If you wish splendour and joy, you will. If you wish damnation because you feel deserved, you will. If you wish to return to the canvas, you will not.

Souls move together in each life, like a herd. We know each other now because we knew each other before. Each of us were friends, lovers and enemies. The phenomena of eternity.

We are flawed because there would be no other reason to continue. Distractions are also a test for you, given by you. The ones who fall behind, who do damage, are children. Nothing more or less. They should not be praised or pitied. You know how long that path will be. And it will take many years or lifetimes for them to see but wish them well on the journey that all of us had to take.

What you experience in the afterlife, is only for you to know. I don't know for certain what you will see and feel, but if you are alive, then you will know more than I.

"The Devil inside, the Devil inside, every single one of us has the Devil inside" (INXS)

Lucifer is a symbol, a category for you to better understand the fluidity of existence. Like all other Divine entities, they are representative of virtues for you to choose, to adapt or discard. The power of choice is your fundamental right.

Demons and angels are figments of your mind's way of trying to understand itself. Such as untold scores of souls, figments of Akashi trying to understand itself. If you speak intent, they are intangible terms.

Heaven and Hell are not separate planes, nor are they on Earth. They live within you. You're your own angels and demons. Any good or misfortune that befalls you is sometimes out of one's control. But what is your ability to handle it? If you run from your demons, they grow larger, If you fight them, then you become them. But if you master yourself, then you are king.

If evil did have a face, it would be one of beauty and innocence.

Management of demon thoughts are here for that. Again, management of demons is the key to unlock the higher doors of existence. Sometimes it's tricky to figure out which ones need management, since they shapeshift into other issues that need attention. Sadly, the ones that cause the most grief and shame is why so few are willing to face them. But remember, those feelings are their way of deterring you from your self-mastery.

You figure it out. Akashi is God, Akashi is Lucifer. Akashi is the same across. It's me and you. Akashi is pull and push inside and outside. Akashi is stupid and intellectual, as it is war and peace. There is no opposite to The All as there is no name for non-existence.

Aggression is not a thing to be exorcised or abhor. It's part of you, as much as love is. You must manage your demons and angels, because if one were to dominate the other, then it will always be you who suffers.

What is the difference between Animal and Human Souls?

No difference. There's no cats, no snakes, no human soul- it's totally pure. Those former states are gone, except, the only difference is the wisdom and experience gained to aid in the advancement of that self.

Cats and dogs express love differently from a physical to soul level, same as some humans and non-terrestrials. My expression of love is unlike the kin beside me. What matters is that expression.

Animals are not masters or servants to any other animal, but two souls can arrange their roles for each other.

I asked Mezreth whether the massive diversity of art and music styles here are unique and unmatched.

Elzona is a world even my kin question why we decided to add our children on its face. That world's secrets lay deeper than her core. It is a very strange world, there are far more mysteries there than on Earth. The Ezoni (guardians of Elzona much like humans are guardians of Earth) have unmatched diversity in their art and much of their inspirations comes from the dynamic, wonderful and terrifying mysteries of their beloved world: Elzona. Why do they create so much? Because they can create, whereas humans gave themselves permission to destroy.

I asked Mezreth whether becoming wrapped up in fighting all the ills and injustices of this chaos is a healthy path to travel towards.

To quote "if you stare in the abyss, the abyss stares back." The pull is strong, its magnetic and lights a fire for justice, but it does not mean that one is immune to its effects of the downward spiral. You're here not only to protect and learn, but also to enjoy. Stop taking life so seriously.

The massive diversity of life on Earth

The only extremes on Earth are the psychological, you live in a cooking pot of dangerous and beautiful. These extremes breed extremes. However, don't mistake this as a negative, it is essential for you to find the balance within yourselves and understand why. Only then can you understand us.

The First Language on Earth

The first language is thought, understanding oneself and one's surroundings to communicate these concepts beyond telepathy is beholden to thought like mathematics is beholden to logic. The first language is the tongue of the soul.

Do Aliens believe in God?
Some think it's creation. Some think it's intelligence. Some think it is destruction and some think it's essence. All correct and all are Akashi. We are all garments of Akashi. Life has always been here.

****

2. Living in the Material World

There are many hidden places on Earth. You need to know where you come from before you can take another step forward.

Measuring our past through technology … The merit of sophistication is not technology, it's awareness. Earth's history is far richer and deeper than the bones it has left behind. Constructing a story, no matter how thorough you analyse and uncover every buried piece, is only a story. You may know how these great creatures walked, what they ate, but have you ever asked what they thought? Did they have a language? Did they have their own Elders? Did they have a culture and laws they abided by? What did they see when they saw their own reflections in the mirrored waters? What did they feel when the sun's warmth touches their backs or when the stars winked at them? Do you ask who they were instead of what they were? We miss them.

When did humans first appear … there are many answers to this popular question, not one of them is true, yet all are correct. Consider this one of many answers, it will take another several hundred millennia for a human to walk on this freshly formed Earth.

Humans walked to cities from the caves, then from the cities back to the caves. On and on this cycle continued and will continue for a few more times.

We only use 15% of our brain … Yes, but you can learn how to use more parts. You have the potential for psionics. However, with the right training and manifesting many more doors will fly open.

The Dreaming Story, the Seven Sisters of the Pleiades, is it all about genetics?

Parts of you are. You were never fully evolved, but you are not entirely made by the hands of nature.

There is no hybridization. You are already us.

We will always be monkeys to our forefathers. There's no shame in it.

I asked Mezreth whether Aliens are as psychology diverse and often broken as we are …

Not just the species, not just social groups or movements, but individuals. No two minds are the same in this Universe. The Ascended are the ones who believe they are heavy, while the heavy believe they are ascended. With that: chaos is born. And wherever there is life, there will be chaos. Indulge in this gift.

All things that have consciousness affect consciousness.

Our Neighbours, the trees, birds and rocks …

One tree is simple. Pulled apart molecule by molecule, the lifeform is almost mechanical. Just like a single neuron. However, when you bundle them, a connection forms, information is exchanged and assimilated to the point where they begin to change themselves in the universal world around them. That one tree is so much more than it was before. It is part of a web and the stronger the web, the greater their song.

Trees, like biological life, are technically a cosmic rarity. Only technically because there's no biological life on Mars and Uranus, Jupiter, Pluto, Mercury. It's a majority that don't have biological life. However, in worlds with biological life, trees are not a biological rarity in that scope. It's true trees on

Earth are biologically unique, like on Elzona, like on Xann and many more.

The trees on Earth were meant to evolve to a greater consciousness biosphere. However, they are sadly putting in efforts to adapt to modern meddling to the naked eye. Trees appear to be mere mechanical organisms, simple and unassuming. However, they can communicate across a whole continent to many different organisms faster, and more effectively than the phone. The biological internet.

Why are there no undomesticated dead birds found in the bush?

The world is a large place. It moves, even the invisible walls shift on the rock and water. For every known place in this world, there are a thousand hidden places.

Why do all animals/birds run or fly together without colliding or stampeding?

The living and the dead ride the waves of the sea of consciousness. We all feel it, but not all know it. It's part of the invisible orchestra of the universe. In some places, the music is mute, while in other places, the music is full. Earth has a song, but it's a pity only a few can hear it.

Life is not restricted to just biological lifeforms. There is far more life out there than you believe. Life existed here long before organic life. Everything is affected by something, and that energy embeds itself into anything close enough with enough years of energy. A simple pebble can hold enough information to summon a soul and a song.

3. Hominids, Genes and Australian Archaeology

The others (hominids) aren't extinct. They have biologically survived into the soup of humanity. Cast away the illusion of uniqueness. There are many worlds who consider themselves to be the only ones like them. Each one of them, like humanity, are a blend and are surviving. They and you are living dreams of ancient genius. You assume you are a singular thing, but you already were many things long before you became humans. We were all born to different stars. But each of us came from the same place.

The other types have never become extinct. They survived in modern humans. Your biological tools allowed you to prevail many changes, and they were given to you by nature and by us. Remember, we blended ingredients, but nature incubated.

Conflict is what drives a soul to change. For better or worse, there was conflict, but there was also peace. However, when these groups fell in love with their greatness, the conflicts turned to wars, and any semblance of peace was the first to become extinct.

There have been a few that have altered your development. Our original model, what my kin intended for you, was different from what you are now. You have also been touched by the Zanashj and those that live outside.

You were moulded by many different hands over many ages, but sometimes, nature would take its course. After every million years, my kin would come and look. However, in recent times our other children (Zanashj) had a hand in your development. They were grand and their flesh crafting was unmatched for an age, but their folly was a greed and grew too comfortable in luxury. Their influence spread across many worlds, but after one small poor choice, they became brittle and ultimately, shattered.

How are we different from animals?

The belief that humans are singular is the only difference. Arrogant ignorance is what makes you distinguished.

4. Mezreth: Up Close and Personal

We don't have a body.

From the beginning, my kin could do both. Some choose permanence of one. We all age, but only a few of us have chosen to die. Be grateful for your brief lives, for you can transcend faster and experience divinity sooner.

I was born in a vacuum. You were born on stone. Where the vacuum and stone are, is not relevant. Since we are born here in this Universe, I have no regrets in my coming here, but I'm not void of regrets.

Without pain we cannot know joy or boundaries. We eat and sleep if we choose to do so.

We copied some of our form over to our children. You adopted your own features over time and impressed what you desire into art, as did we. Vanity is not exclusive to humans. You call many beings angels. I have been referred to as an angel, also a fallen one, neither wrong nor right.

When Mezreth incarnated into an Earthly body …

It doesn't matter what new life soul incarnates into. They will never be able to remember every memory of their past lives. However, one must be open to the memories peaking through, not shying away. No matter how heartbreaking the memory, the more you will pull away, the less your current mind will be able to remember. There are many reasons why someone cannot recall their past lives. They refuse to do so. They don't understand what they are.

And for others, they have a thick haze wrapped around their soul that stops them. In my old life, I viewed the world through a keyhole. I was ignorant by accident and arrogant by choice. I made many mistakes for my soul to learn from. But those mistakes are being paid by others. That's why I am here. My perspective was narrow then, so it may be wider now.

xxxxxxxxxxxxxxxxxxxxxxxxxxxxxxxxxxxxxxxxxxxxxxxxxxxxx

5. Yowies and Bittars (Hobbits)

They are the last remaining pure Elementals. They are what you could have been, they are wild but aware of you. Their forests are their cities, and the trees are their skyscrapers, but they have been forced to adapt to your growing presence, despite their ferocity, they are aware they are not the apex predator on Earth. That horrid crown is on humans.

They are of earth and have always been, and wilfully always will be. Both of your kin came from One many millennia ago. You two are cousins, but one has been favoured by the Grandmother.

They live for 130 years in this realm, barring illness or injury or a broken heart.

Some groups simply need to be certain heights. Consider this: if humans are lions, then wildmen are tigers. Consider one's lone survival in the wilds of Earth, would you need size, height and strength on your side?

You two were nearby for a long time-and once you two were friends. However, one believed they were greater, productive and a more useful friend, and one day, that friend single-handedly changed the world without thinking about the other. Make no mistake, humans may have arrogance as their greatest sin, but the wildmen can hold grudges that out last any stone.

They've walked the woods, deserts, and snow longer than you. They have met many curiosities about Earth and learnt her secrets. They are aware of another that shares the world, but they became afraid and dug themselves deeper in their walls. And that fear that was once poisonous to them, has become a disease for all others on Earth.

Of course, if you pay attention, you can understand them.

Some acknowledge they may exist but assume they are more primitive and less intelligent.
The wildmen ponder the same question about you.

Does their voice contain magic qualities?

It's a blend of many things. The sound effects the atom, the atom can affect itself. Remember how delicate one becomes when they are afraid, remember how dangerous they become.

Uncle Donny insists there are two types of Yowies, one is physical the other in spirit form.

The Old Ones eventually became blended with the curtain.

Why do they hide from us?

They didn't want to be infected.

Can Humans and Yowies cross-incarnate?

Of course.

Why do Yowies mistrust Aliens more than Humans?

Before there were wildmen and humans, there was One. Our Children, who were misguided, sought to be Gods of the stars. They came to Earth and saw you and wanted to change you. After some centuries, humans were born, while the wildmen were forced to retreat. Since then, when they see us in the skies, they believe it's the old, terrible times again.

Then there are the Little Versions (Nimbinjas, Bittars, 'Hobbits')

Those beings are as clever as adults, but their hearts are as children. If you are gifted to their frequency, they will welcome you if they are confident in your intent. Like their larger and more potent cousins, the little men are also aware of the viciousness of grown men. However, the little men know this wasn't always so. They aspire to bond with fledgelings, in the hopes they can subdue this terrifying aspect of men.

6. Lemuria and Atlantis

Australia was the source of inspiration for all human cultures.

Art, language and thought came from Lemuria.

Lemuria is still here and making choices either for the ending or against the ending of the book.

Lemuria was the first and one of the few remaining ancient civilisations, unlike Atlantia and the many societies that have come and gone throughout memory, Lemuria will still be here until the last cell dies.

Lemuria never lived without the wand and her wielders.

All modern humans have ties to the golden age of Atlantis. Although not all were Atlanteans. And if Atlantia was the clock and Alkhem was the jewel, then Lemuria was the wand.

The freehold of Lemuria stretched from the North Pacific Islands all the way to the shores of Africa. Lemuria was not a city or nation. It was a world of its own. Atlantis found their way to the crocodile's nose for many millennia, until they were judged and ultimately expelled.

Atlantia had tens of millions spanning across the island. Lemuria never reached over a million. Lemuria was a place to visit, not to live.

Modest tribes were scattered. They had nexus points to discuss and exchange. These points were great places for refuge, but none did make them home. It was home to

Lemuria and her invisible children; each nexus point was equally spread for each community. There is a reason why the wise seek solace and the obtuse seek equal company. This is a reason why each member of the pack has a face, and the herd is faceless. Lemuria knew this because Lemuria had told them.

Lemuria greets visitors through her jaw of judgment. It can take a day or a thousand lifetimes, but all are ultimately judged. Make no mistake, Lemurians do not make this choice. They are mere speakers for the land. Lemuria understood something beyond what her guests could see. She read the book and cast her choice in favour for the events to come or against. Never forget Lemuria, she still judges.

Why did Lemuria never fall from its pedestal?

The one thing countless cultures failed to achieve is that they imprinted themselves into the land. They took its power from it. Instead, they (Lemurians) nurtured it, tended to it, until it became its own face. And in turn, the land gave them Law.

All visitors (including Aliens) had to pass through the jaws and into the belly of Lemuria. The Lemurians, who had been there for countless millennia, were still seen as visitors. Yet their judgment allowed them to stay and learn.

The ancient Alkhemites knew about the Lemurians for many millennia, but they had especially known about the strained relationship between Atlanteans and Lemurians. The Alkhemites sought to resurrect that old friendship, and so they had — for a time.

The Lemurians saw a shadow behind the Atlanteans. It had dawned on them that these people were on a clock and that their sun will be setting soon, forever.

Atlantia was a clock, but Atlanteans were deaf to the ticking. The Lemurians could hear it and they saw how deaf Atlanteans were and the Lemurians desperately sympathised.

The Fall…

All worlds are special, but a word of caution the Atlanteans also believed they were special.

The crystals may have stopped Atlanteans breath, but Atlantia was dead long before.

Aliens living in Atlantis … There was a time when that separation really began this issue. In Atlantis, we lived together here and now as the culture changed. So did their hearts and minds, paranoia and pride ate away at the Atlanteans. They wanted to be stars. Warnings were given but the stars closed their eyes and then they remained closed.

In times of Atlantis, we were together, and even before that. All peoples in the interstellar community were too young to appreciate each other. So, they returned to their cradles to grow a little more. Lots of lanterns. I was already lost, for the moon guardians lost themselves.

Hubris. The taste of wonder became an addiction in our observations, even in our time; a great civilisation is the one that humbles itself and sees its own limitations before improving on them. As is for the collective, as is for the soul, as is for the cosmos.

Atlantia' Surrogate Child: Egypt

The Atlantean cataclysm was sparked when the island died, but the survivors rode the waves of destruction for centuries — leading to deaths of communication, cities, and whole cultures into the After.

The few who were away survived, they mourned by attempting to reclaim their former glory. They never could.

Egypt was home for many civilisations over the millennia, all had unique languages, philosophies, and ways of seeing. However, all succumbed to greed and the lust for power. Despite their great ability to ward off Atlantean survivors, they eventually became the new richest nation in the world and yet again, they have been tainted by the same old thing.

7. The Rings from Atlantis and Lemuria

Those rings were made for those who embodied Lemuria. They were parted and scattered across the landscapes, each piece becoming greater than what was before and the Atlanteans realised this.

They're only tools. They maximise whatever traits you have, and the larger your ego is, the larger it becomes from their monstrous power; they will only add to that vicious cycle. Those tools are also part of the exam, and the right choice is to leave them be. Atlanteans had similar tools that allowed their empire to flourish and look what happened.

We have spoken often about the three rings from Atlantis and that they had a seminal role in destroying Atlantis. What went wrong and why were two buried in Australia at Hill End (33 degrees south of the Equator) and the third in Scotland?

They went to places that most of the ancient world feared to tread. The rings had no choice in what their fates had become. Their masters and keepers had gifted them to the worst people, allowing their magic to enhance and unbury

their darkest natures of their holder's souls. Over and over. Enhance, destroy, absorb-grow. Enhance, destroy, absorb-grow. Their makers invented an incurable disease.

Was permission from the Hill End Original tribes obtained before burial?

Those rings were ripped from dead hands, and once it was realised what they truly were, they were given to those who would never use it and had the power to willingly forget that power.

8. Edgar Cayce and Dolores Cannon

My and kin and I speak to anyone who needs to listen.

Dolores spoke of the change and of "two trains" that each person has to choose from. You must remember that every passenger can leap out of the moving train at any time.

It's of the soul, not physicality.

Dolores also spoke of disease and sickness being something we should never experience and that it is merely unfamiliar information codes.

That statement is technically correct, but its pregnant with misconceptions. All matter contains data, but the key is how the reader decodes it.

Cayce spoke of the varying times when a soul enters the foetus. It can depend on how quick the soul decides to occupy the foetus. The most common time for a soul entering a growing pineal gland in a human host averages at around two months. But there are many different organisms with different gestation periods. But this is specifically talking about humans and also depends on how steadfast that soul is to actually occupy.

Some tend to want to linger around until the right time comes around the potential parent and potential body, and then links in with it.

Cayce believes all souls were created at the same time. Our souls are broken and forged, absorbed and separated at all times. There is no beginning. There is no end. The only time is a circle of eternity. A piece of stone, as it is, may be a mere eon, but the energy of the stone is timeless. Just as my soul may be an eon, the age of my energy is forever.

The only time Mezreth challenged or qualified their work was in relation to Cayce's belief our character and fate is substantially influenced by the twelve houses of the Zodiac.

Don't worry. He is not right in his conclusion. But you must remember the outer universe is a reflection of the inner universe. And if the heart bends the hand follows. The universe moves in spite for you, in love for you, and always around you.

The only universe that we have any semblance of control over is the one on the inside. And if you can master that, then the rest follows.

9. Pyramids and Pylons

It (pyramids) was introduced by the Zanashj, but human engineers and crafters adjusted the structure to fit this planet.

Yes, many cultures contributed their own desires on these machines, long after Atlanteans became a memory.

When the Plateau was merely land, hundreds of minds came together to advance their understanding of reality-to push the limits of knowledge. They almost succeeded. They had to invent things specially for the project. Many scientists, scholars, engineers, and priests had their lives dominated by their obsessive wants to make their mark. They wanted to witness the wonders of the universe act before them-in service to them, but they failed and now, all of them have been forgotten by their descendants.

The Plateau was a representation of human ingenuity, brilliance, and moral cooperation. Every human of every background had their lives immortalised in those stones. The Plateau was what the Atlanteans wanted for the future-but the bricks crumbled all the same with their morals.

The Great Pylons of Old have been misunderstood since the Fall (Atlantean Cataclysm). Many civilisations tried rebuilding their own versions in homage and worship to their mystique. The Pylons were the key to an untold future of the ancient world. Their light had never been given the chance to brighten the world. A tragedy for those who understood their potential.

Can they still work ... They were designed in a way to remove the need of current conventional power generating methods. The pylons are now active, but they are on standby. Their shape, mass, alignment and the material perfectly curated for the place they were built on: an astral nexus point.

It can be used again, you have an abundance of materials but lack the knowing.

A single pylon cannot, but an operating cluster can. Many ancient structures have fallen into decay and ruin. Some are still active, but you need to be in our minds to know how to use them.

There are many ways to construct these structures, provided what the builder aims to do with it and what purpose they serve. Some were fitted to generate energy, others to process water, others to bridge communication grids and stabilise dynamic spatial sectors. To put it simply, if the builder wants to enhance their own energetic pathways (of their own body), they can construct a copper and/or crystalline pyramid frame with their bare hands before recharging and regenerating in the small alcove.

The Pyramids on Mars ... Nothing about Mars was an accident, but it had become a tragedy. Mars was our kin's first choice to seed — -it was a paradise until our genius was hijacked by pride.

We never left Mars, nor Saturn, nor her moons and Jupiter's.

Stone Henge ... It was an attempt to build another type of pylon for unique tasks, but the builders lacked the precision, logistics, and materials. Make no mistake, the engineers were descendants of Alkhemites and Atlanteans long after the Fall. They held the memory of those times but failed at recalling the wisdom.

The Standing Sones site in Australia ... The Standing Stones are older than the ruins of Stone Henge. Their power relied on the grounds they sat on, but their sequence and embedded ancient energy connected them to our Little Siblings. The First Language (which is found on these rocks) was made by man, but the first thought came from the stars.

The Failed Manhattan Project ... Phasing technology is one of the hallmarks of a civilisation ready for interstellar travel, but before that civilisation can join our interstellar community, they must be aware of the devastating dangers of it. If phasing is misused, nuclear contamination would be a dream of the past.

10. The Kariong Hieroglyphs were first engraved ... in the twilight days of the first tongue.

That place is grander and deeper than what is said. The signs aren't the magic, they merely point to it.

Of who was and will be, how many times it will happen and when time rolls into nothingness. It speaks about an era and people who had arrived there for the first time, only to realise they were there many times before.

They were added by the same people who returned over many years. For every one thing you see there, there are a thousand things you don't.

The tragedy is any changes to all land and water affect nexus points. However, considering that they are dwindling in number and power, this is one site you cannot afford to lose. Unless you wish to delay your progression again.

What tools were used ... As delicate as a pen, but harder than steel. The first women know.

Aunty Beve said there is Egyptian and older hieroglyphs written by Original people ... They were far from the first who came to learn from the first men, but they were one of the last. She is a Lemurian soul, she was born with knowledge, but it took much of her life to understand it.

Why did the Egyptians come ... When the Atlanteans were blinded, the others seized an opportunity to save themselves from them.

Everyone knew about Lemuria.

The sacred Grandmother tree is claimed by its critics to be a lie and a mere tourist attraction ... There are mouths where ears should be.

11. Aliens on and near Earth, why ...

We have been here since day one. It's a mixture of personal compassion as well as honouring certain alliances of the past. Humans have been in contact with us for a very, very long time. We believe humans have the potential to reclaim those old times, to reclaim those old ways to survive these new ways. Humans have a mixture of resentment for the old, but there's also a fear of the new. Constant fear and anxiety will only ever lay down a path of darkness. We are trying to change that.

Mixing and merging here, there and everywhere. We've been together for a long time, so long that the idea of ours and yours has lost meaning. We have lost meaning. There are ancient human remains dotted around the Cosmos posing equal mysteries. You and they, and we-ours, yours, and theirs, all meaningless-all is the same. Origin is the same for all beings.

All forms of life see the universe through a single pair of eyes and judge actions based on their personal experience. It doesn't matter how high the growth of perspective somebody has, it is still within their narrow confines of their perceptions. It doesn't matter how high they are. Even for us, the sky is the limit. It doesn't matter how rich or poor your life experiences were, management of attitude and responses to situations is vital. You will never truly 100% absolutely see the Universal Truth in its full entirety because you will always perceive some bias. We have seen the whole Universe and each of us emphasise different aspects. Our own values became watered down because of an abundance of time. Some of us were infected with apathy. Peaceful, yes. But we stopped wandering and became lost.

Earth has been a home to many beings. Some have been transient and were born there. They have left in crafts and others walked away from the world. You will reunite with them again. They wait by the shining dog Sirius.

What we offer is chances and choices. The only hindrance is the blind fear of consequences. There is no consequence that you cannot learn from. And we will ensure you have the opportunity to do so.

We want to share this interstellar community with you once again. But we need assurances you will open your eyes. If you cannot then you cannot, then it will only be you who suffers.

Why wait, why not come down now and guide us now... We are. We're doing it now, as we've always done. We won't burst into the bedroom while a child holds a gun. It's a recipe for further heartache. I've seen the consequences before. If you want us to do more, you must reach us halfway.

Earth is not their (Zanashj) home, but it was part of a dominion.

The Zanashj have been humbled by their arrogance, their assumption that they sat at the top of the pyramid in their sphere of influence, made them forgetful and small. Their weaknesses were discovered and exploited, and the dominion on many worlds shrunk until their influence caved in. Earth was also in their dominion, but you (humans) cast them away at the right time. Zanashj have never recovered from those days, nor do they intend repeating them. Can you say the same for yourselves?

There's been many species on and around Earth, like many other worlds. It's not unique. There's a long history with humans and Zanashj, but Zanashj are not Reptilian, though their appearance can trick the inexperienced eye. They were shapeshifters taking faces of many to adapt to many environments. They made poor choices but seek redemption from those they have damaged. Some are here now, learning from the same school as you.

What of the motives of the Reptilians and Draconians ... We represent only some of the factions. Your closets neighbours, the Xannians, they see, they fear you as you are now. But the needs on why they choose to risk themselves may frighten you. In the beginning, their motivations on

befriending you are of survival, but you would gain much from that relationship should you master your fear. All they want is an exchange.

What can you tell us about the no-foreheads beings we have and have also examined in-situ? They were our siblings. Our younger kin. They left their cradle, their home, to travel for the love of curiosity. Then they made friends, on and on they would go, but after ages, friendships broke, and alliances took over. Our little siblings got too involved and lost heart after some time, they abandoned their goals and returned home. Never wanting to return again and never wanting to leave again.

Revisiting Mars ... Mars was long before Earth. Mars was our first choice, but through our choices, Earth became our only option.

Life on Mars ... is mostly introduced. **What Brought it to Extinction ...** we did.

We never left Mars.

The Official Government Response ... They lie through the truth. You are being prepared for a new fear. A kind of fear that will overshadow the one for a mere disease.

There are factions even within the shadows. The lines have blurred and have broken, but they know they are being watched by you and us.

12. The Ceremony at Uluru December 2020- For any who are unaware of this seminal ceremony we will provide a brief summary of what happened. If seeking a more detailed account, we recommend the reader go to our web site where the many written articles discuss the specifics.

We first heard talk that the most important ceremony conducted on this planet was to take place at Uluru on December 20, 2020, about five years before the gathering was held. We were given the same details, date, location, number of people needed to supplement what the Elders did at Uluru along with the global consequences, from multiple sources.

It was claimed to be transformational, in that the Earth would cleanse itself. The Schumann Resonance, which is a measurement of the Earth's 'heartbeat,' would dramatically accelerate and every animal and form of life, bar one species, would be part of this ascension. Alas, as a collective, humans are the sole architects of all the grief, poison and chaos that blights this planet, and because of this litany of poor choices must earn a 'ticket to ride.'

Granted for the fifteen to twenty million people who joined in this ceremony that was one step in right direction, but it is the first of many and of itself needing much more. All of these people took a leap of faith through participating in something that was entirely lacking in supporting empirical evidence, but what happened during and directly after is real and factual.

We have photographs, videos and reports of events seen that fill that gap in solid evidence. We have film of Uluru exploding in a ball of white light that covers the sky, which took place four minutes after the ceremony began. Equally we have film of an incredibly slow-moving object tracking across the rock at the same time. It makes its way to an intense blue patch in the clouds after sunset; the horizon is a washed out pale blue yet there above was an intensely vibrant blue hole in the sky.

What is both challenging and convincing is the film was taken by a person who is legally deemed to be blind and did not see this object while filming. As he scans the sky primarily filming the multiplicity of colours in the clouds, he captured the object moving through the clouds on two occasions. Yet what is extremely compelling is when the camera pans past the blue patch the object is not readily visible. Or so it would seem, but one person viewing this film slowed it down and on the fourth frame on the fifty-ninth and sixtieth second the object reappears, but is not seen in either of the other three frames for both the fifty-ninth and sixtieth seconds. It vanishes, appears, then vanishes and reappears again, all within a two second gap.

For any who think it could be some sort of very slow-moving plane or helicopter hovering, we have a radar map of every known flying object at 7:32 pm, showing one, and it is commercial jet 400 kilometres to the east and nothing anywhere else. The last helicopter flight that evening at Uluru landed at 5 pm and after that the pad was closed. No helicopter flights are allowed after five o'clock and equally, it is forbidden at any time to fly over the big red rock.

We also have a huge collection of photos from all over the planet of bizarre columns of light, including a second deep blue patch in the skies over America which seems to validate the Hopi Dreaming story of the two "Katchinas," who are two Alien brothers who were prophesised to appear to announce this planetary ascension simultaneously in the Northern and Southern Hemisphere. So too, do we have film of the final Hopi sign of the Red Eye hovering in the sky.

And while focussed upon the sky above, the sky just before a rock ceremony was held about 15 kilometres from Uluru was a dark grey and actually was lightly raining while the rocks were being positioned. But after the twenty minutes of group meditation and sun setting, it wasn't just the deep blue patch that captured the attention of those seated in the dirt, but the clouds above. We asked the chief security guard if she had ever seen such a huge array of colours in the same grey clouds. "Absolutely not," nothing ever before came close, and knowing the sun had set everyone was watching, photographing and filming this display.

So powerful was the impact of the ceremony at Uluru, which was intended to activate what the Elders referred to as the "magic box," quite a few people, including my son Evan, literally felt the Earth shaking. These events, and many others, accompanied this sacred ceremony in heralding in a change in Earthly circumstances.

However, as mentioned earlier being there and participating is a great start but that alone does not guarantee any form of admission when the change comes, so much more is needed. Very, very, few humans living on this planet are ready or prepared for what is coming down the line. To that end, Mezreth has shared with us guidelines, suggestions and paths to consider that will greatly assist in each soul's progress and readiness. While obeying the agreed directive that most Aliens abide by, in not directly interfering, many can if they wish dismiss this all as being Lea's imagination, or perhaps her deliberate lies and manipulations, and refuse to read or engage. That is their choice, they can ignore every word presented and suffer the consequences.

Needless to say, the Aliens who have taken such a long-term interest in this planet were also part of this global interaction and experiment which is now reaching the final stages. Mezreth's observations and comments only amplify how important what took place is to not only the residents of this planet, but it extends everywhere and impacts on everything, not just on this planet but that ascension resonates to every planet and constellation.

xxxxxxxxxxxxxxxxxxxxxxxxxxxxxxxxxxxxxxxxxxxxxxxxxxxxxxx

Uluru is the soul of Lemuria. There's the future you now inhabit, and it is where it all began and will all end.

The ceremony was a landmark in many ways because it proved not just to humans, but to us that you can work together for a common goal. And when humans connect, and stick to something, you have that common desire in that moment, it has affected the planet. Can you imagine what eight billion people can create? Imagine how many strides forward you can achieve with this. It was a test, and you passed with flying colours. But there are many more challenges ahead. Can you remember that solution for the next challenge, we wonder? Fifteen million opened the door, but it takes the world to change the world.

Humans are not the only ones that have hummed to Uluru. We bond with you in many ways, not just with speakers. We want you to see the Universe from where we are.

It doesn't matter how far you are, Uluru can hear your song and Lemuria will respond, Lemuria always responds.

This is a test for all times and all manner of beings, not just humans, but beings. This fine balance is something we have all walked and we continue to walk for the sake of our continual evolutions. There will never be a time of true serenity in life; life itself is chaos by default. What the point is, is to find everlasting and beneficial chaos. This is also traumatic for a soul and in turn, trauma for the body. Find your sense and then you will find your purpose. The challenge is realising your reality, your purpose will never match another's. So, to impose one's reality and compare one's to another inhibits the soul, the person's ability to find purpose, to find self. The inner universe is the only thing that exists. All beyond is a mere reflection.

You make the right choice. The exam is to see if you are going to make the right choice. Every one of those choices are bought with consequences. You've always been at crossroads, but now those crossroads cannot be ignored or left until later. Apathy won't save you.

Don't lie to yourselves.

Change comes every day, but it will take a million right changes to reach the ending you wish. However, don't assume it will be an age free of wrongs.

Souls will still be able to reincarnate, but few will be able to successfully pass through. Those who recall their lessons may re-enter, but those who wilfully forget, will not. This leaves the door open for them to come back when they have.

The soul departs to a place for reflection. The body returns to the land so that the soul may have a chance to live again. Today you are breaking that cycle.

We want from you the same thing Akashi wants. How can one be all without being one?

If you have correctly nurtured a person, you have saved the world. The exam is your life, and the results are the lives that come after. The only failure is the one where you repeat the same mistakes in the assumption that you will pass. For now, the passing grade is to avoid making the same mistakes in this century.

The promise is the answer to the question of why you came here this time. To see spring, you must endure the winter. You have never seen spring, you came close once before, and maybe you will see it this time.

The next five observations made relate to the acceleration of the Schumann Resonance ...

The bumps and peaks will continue to ensure that you will remember the lessons so we're going to keep that pressure to see if you can do it again. The ceremony was a lesson but what we are doing now is the real test. And the results of this test will prove that you can not only control the Schuman Resonance, but your fates, too.

It was mostly you when you tuned in. At the same time, it was uncomfortable to feel its effects. Not only can you turn it up and down, but you can also balance it for yourselves. We also added a spark to it. It was a way for us to see you and you see us.

The turmoil is akin to what happened before, but to see spring, you need to understand how to overcome it forever. This is the best way for each individual to have this foundation laid. Without this, you will lack the wisdom for future challenges.

Beginnings and ends happen within every beat.

There is nothing for those who side with fear over opportunity. Choices define existence as there is a consequence to each, even if you believe you made the right one. Like most civilisations that have come before you, you have come to a point where choice is no longer an option. Don't worry. You will overcome any challenge if you remember and work together as a group. Hearing you say that you can change is always lovely when you are safe and content, but we wonder if that will extend when you are faced with danger.

Change is ugly, uncomfortable and brutal. If it's pleasant, then the wrong thing is changing and it's often the thing that will be your downfall. You have living memories that are equipped with this knowledge and understanding. Don't ask us, ask them.

This time this will defeat you, but you will not die. When these days pass, you will marvel at a strength you never knew you had, then and only then will you know. You will know these days were a gift.

The ones who go on will be changed for the better as one may imagine but there will come a worse time, remember the cost of arrogance! Humility is the lantern in the dark. Yes, you are open to vulnerability, but you will be seen as true and trusted. Knowing and embracing your strengths and weaknesses may bring you higher. But you asked what happens to those without lanterns: they remain untouched, unseen, and blind in the dark. The cruellest karma that can befall a soul is nothing, they don't grow, they don't change, they linger in life, but they are already dead.

The Big Bang was a point of change, but life existed before. Like the many other cataclysms before, when life decided to change. We can still see the waves of the Big Bang rippling out in the black and its many predecessors. Life changes. It's a must for the Universe; if it stagnates its consciousness falters. Don't fear the death of life as you know it. Fear the death of challenge.

Is the Earth the only planet transcending? No, far from the only one. Of course, there will be another world that will offer the same challenges for the young. This is merely the Earth's turn.

After the change ... A new set of problems but you won't be able to solve them without moulding the tools from your current issues. Don't worry about tomorrow.

Those in control, were they aware of this ceremony and the implications? They know and some unwittingly participated. The tsunami crashed and now the tides are reeling all into the sea.

In ancient times did humans travel through space? Humans too walked from this world, back and forth, but there will come a time when humans walk away from Earth for the last time.

First Set of Transcripts

Transcript One
Chapter 12

Steve:

I know E.T.s are here, but why would they bother to come here?

Now what I'm getting out of that is it's not so much coming here as they were here before we were. And they've seen now in our growth at least 15 hominids running around 300,000 years ago and found another hominid in China a couple of days ago which has got a much bigger brain than ours. So somehow, they chose sapiens among all the different hominids. I find it quite interesting that there is that sort of parental link because obviously genes were crossed. Now there's two things I really want to see if we can cover. One's the ceremony, and the other is the Schumann Resonance. Mezreth is aware that ceremony took place at Uluru. And we were given a minimum number of participants which I never told anyone beforehand that we had to reach, which we exceeded by nearly fifteen million. I've got a suspicion E.T.s had some sort of either observer or participant involvement. Well, was it successful? And if it was, what did it actually do?

Mezreth:

We have been here since day one. It's a mixture of parental compassion as well as honouring certain alliances of ancient past. Humans have been in contact with us for a very, very long time. We believe humans have the potential to reclaim those old times, to reclaim those old ways to survive these new days. Humans have a mixture of resentment for the old, but there's also a fear of the new. Constant fear and constant anxiety will only ever lay down a path of darkness. We are trying to change that.

The ceremony was a landmark in many ways because it proved to not just humans, but to us that you can work together for a common goal. And when humans connect, and you stick to something, you have that common desire in that moment, it has affected the planet. Can you imagine what eight billion people can create? Imagine how many strides forward you can achieve with this. It was a test, and you passed with flying colours. But there are many more challenges ahead. Can you remember that solution for the next challenge, we wonder? Fifteen million opened the door, but it takes the world to change the world.

Steve:

So, in other words, what that's done is opened the door. I never actually thought that meant everything was roses. So now let's talk about the Schumann Resonance. It fluctuated massively during the December, 2020 ceremony. Were they involved with that or did humans do that? Or was that something completely independent?

Well, that's quite deep actually. I think that really is something to think about in a lot of respects. Now, with the Schumann Resonance we made an issue of this and there's more of add to it. Evan showed me a read-out where for three days in a row at around about 1:00, the Schumann Resonance was shooting into the forties and fifties. And as we know, it's also gone up to 6000 on one occasion. And as we now know, it's gone up to a level beyond the measurement of any machine. Now I've heard rumours that now the Schumann Resonance is turned on, it's become a plaything for Aliens. Why is it still changing so much?

This is the whole point of this exercise. We know about that now. Is there a point in the near future where many souls incarnate here right now, will not be able to reincarnate on the planet because the frequency will be so high, that if they did, they'd perish on the Earth?

Mezreth:

It was mostly you when you tuned in. At the same time, it was uncomfortable to feel its effects. Not only can you turn it up and down, but you can also balance it for yourselves. We also added our spark to it. It was a way for us to see you and you to see us.

The bumps and spikes will continue to ensure that you remember the lessons so we're going to keep that pressure to see if you can do it again. The ceremony was a lesson but what we are doing now is the real test. And the results of this test will prove that you can not only control the Schuman Resonance, but your fates, too.

Souls will be able to reincarnate, but few will successfully pass through. Those who recall their lessons may re-enter, but those who wilfully forget, will not. This leaves the door open for them to come back when they have.

Steve:

It's very much like I said, there were two lessons we had to get here. One was to learn about magic and love which means you're playing well in the playground, instead of spitting at each other. And the second one was to learn why we are here. The reason for everything and what seems to be clear to me from what you're saying there, is there has to be some idea of what both love and magic is. But there also has to be some real understanding of the purpose, and reason why people are here. Now, for the last question: as you said, some won't be able to incarnate back here. Some can come, some can't. As for the ones who can come back here or stay here after that point in time, what comes next for the ones who do stay? Is there any vision for the future they have?

Mezreth:

There is nothing for those who side with fear over opportunity. Choices define existence as there is a consequence to each, even if you believe you made the right one. Like most civilizations that have come before you, you have come to a point where choice is no longer an option. Don't worry. You will overcome any challenge if you remember and work together as a group. Hearing you say that you can change is always lovely when you are safe and content, but we wonder if that will extend when you are faced with danger.

Transcript Two
Chapter 13

Steve:

We've mentioned this before, that the zebra, who have the same genetic general patterns in face, size and lifestyle – if you've seen one zebra, then you have seen them all. Whereas humans have seven million different faces, different fingerprints, height, style and everything else. Why are humans so distinguishable and unique? What is it that's different about our genes?

That means this genetic mixture that we're talking about relates to what specifically happened with one species of human. Clearly, they've done this elsewhere. It seems to be a common practice. This is not the only place that has happened. Do the Zanashj come from here or do they come from somewhere else?

So, we are a mixed bag from apes and E.Ts. This leads on to the second question which is the primary reason and long-term expectation of this type of genetic hybridization, what's the reason and expectation for it?

Mezreth:

You were moulded by many different hands over many ages, but sometimes, nature would take its course. After every million years, my kin would come and look. However, in recent times, our other children (Zanashj) had a hand in your development. They were grand and their flesh crafting was unmatched for an age, but their folly was a greed and grew too comfortable in luxury. Their influence spread across many worlds, but after one small poor choice, they became brittle and ultimately, shattered.

Earth is not their home, but it was part of a dominion.

There is no hybridization. You are already us.

Steve:

That's the history we've got to discover, isn't it? The long-term purpose is for that curtain to be placed there and for us to realize why. They work with other races for different purposes. Now this is the part I can tick off, in that there was some genetic sharing for a specific reason. Then past that point, we've got two options that are on offer.

The accepted mainstream genetic truth, that we've been told is absolutely right, which is one day a monkey mummy, and a monkey daddy made us. We crawled around on all fours, then we stood up on two legs, then we dribbled a little and then walked into a cave about 40,000 years ago.

And here we are today at the pinnacle of existence on this planet, maybe in the cosmos. That is one version and the second one is that there were earlier times and civilisations and that from the very beginning there was a melding of lines and genes. And we've had times since when we were as advanced technologically and spiritually as we are today, if not more so, then it all fell apart.

After each fall we went back to nature and became hunters and gatherers, then we stumbled back into the system of doing the same mistakes we made earlier. We hoped that the next time we're going to get it right. And we keep doing it again and again, and here we are now preparing for the next instalment. It really has to be one of the two. Our evolution is not the one we see on the science posters of us evolving from earlier hominids like Australopithecus. They are no more than a different species, a bit like all the different monkeys and different primates. So, which one was correct?

Mezreth:

We will always be monkeys to our forbearers. There's no shame in it.

Steve:

I wish that was a little less cryptic. It seems that to our forebears we will always be monkeys, but with the benefit of some intriguing genetic supplements.

We know of Atlantis and Lemuria, and I don't think there's any argument that each empire existed. And if that is so, could you briefly describe their greatest achievements and inherent failings.

He's talking about why it failed, which is, of course, the most important part of this equation, isn't it? Because eventually what's going to come out of this change ahead is another civilization is going to have to live together in some shape or form. Obviously, Atlantis would be the best example of what we need to guard against. And right now, we'd be vying for first place with Atlantis, wouldn't we? Moving forward, from Atlantis to Lemuria. Let's make this more specific so that we get an answer. This time I think it's going to be the same answer. I think I know the answer. Is it the same answer for both of them?

During the ebbs and flows of what's taken place on this planet and it's been a long time, that's obvious, there have been many earlier civilizations and it sounds to me like they've always fallen into the same trap. During this time, an extensive time, what assistance and hindrance did the alien community offer as humans staggered through the destruction in Atlantis and Lemuria, what were they doing to help and guide?

Mezreth:

Hubris. The taste of wonder became an addiction in our observations, even in our own time, a great civilization is the one that humbles itself and sees its own limitations before improving on them as is for the collective, as is for the soul and as is for the cosmos.

Similar.

What we offer is chances and choices. The only hindrance is the blind fear of consequences. There is no consequence that you cannot learn from. And we will ensure you have the opportunity to do so.

Steve:

In fact, that's probably all we have to think about as it is our journey and choices. So, he offers chances and we're fearful of the consequence. Every now and then, you get a person that is stunning with ears to hear like Da Vinci or Tesla. They were not scared of the consequences, were they? They're just committed to taking the chance when it comes along. And that's the difference between nearly all of us. So that's what they've been doing.

But when you do step outside the status quo and see the real truths, it is a blessing and potential curse as one has to also control the ego and sense of importance, for if let to run free there will be consequences.

So special that they saw themselves as first amongst equals, and that is a dangerous road to navigate. What I want to discuss next relates back to the ceremony that took place, which we've agreed was actually a real thing. We don't have to go through and validate that. We know it's now only months away, what advice would he offer to humanity?

Mezreth:

All worlds are special, but a word of caution: Atlanteans also believed they were special.

Change is ugly, uncomfortable and brutal. If it's pleasant, then the wrong thing is changing and it's often the thing that will be your downfall. You have living memories that are equipped with this knowledge and understanding. Don't ask us; ask them.

Transcript Three
Chapter 14

Steve:

My first question is, is it true to say that the alien race also ranges from almost ascended to uncaring and purely self-interested as many of us are today? Is that a fair call? Is that what's happened over there on the other side?

So, wherever it is, life is chaos. Well, that must mean right now on this planet, we are so alive. The question that follows, because it is a now two-part question, how can this be?

Surely the more knowledgeable, the more technologically advanced and having a big picture view of everything, should theoretically make you more aware and compassionate.

That so much of the truth is hidden or stolen on this planet makes things even more difficult here. And that loss of vision and mystical purpose on this planet makes a lot of good people turn into not so good people because they don't have a big picture overview. But elsewhere most Aliens have more of these truths there for the taking. Shouldn't that lead to being selfless, less belligerent, and peaceful? How is it that some of these less caring off-worlders are so ambivalent and sometimes even violent when they shouldn't be? Is there an explanation for how that could be happening?

Mezreth:

Not just the species, not just social groups or movements but individuals. No two minds are the same in this universe. The Ascended are the ones who believe they are heavy, while the heavy believe they are ascended. With that: chaos is born. And wherever there is life, there is chaos. Indulge in this gift.

All forms of life see the universe through a single pair of eyes and judge actions based on their personal experience. It doesn't matter how high the growth of perspective somebody has, it is still within their narrow confines of their own perceptions. It doesn't matter how high they are. Even for us, the sky is the limit. It doesn't matter how rich or poor your life experiences were, management of attitude and responses to situations is vital. You will never truly 100% absolutely see the universal truth in its full entirety because you will always perceive with some bias. We have seen the whole universe and each of us emphasize different aspects. Our own values became watered down because of an abundance of time. Some of us were infected with apathy. Peaceful, yes. But we stopped wandering and became lost.

Steve:

Do all aliens believe in some form of God-like creator? And then to be specific, because I'm aware of the fact the aliens who have taken an interest in human affairs are so numerous, in this area is there a commonality in perspective and understanding of how and who created everything?

What were their intentions and dispositions. And did they use humans or liaise with them? Because that to me is the crucial element in our evolution. I hear stories of both using us sometimes as a slave race and sometimes liaising with us as equal partners. So, what was going on, and who are this mob? Where are they from, what makes them different from us and what are their motivations?

So it's not really part of what this planet is about why we're here and why they're here that is the essential issue. This is supposed to be a place where they're trying to merge everything into one, aren't they? All the differences merge into a common goal. And therefore, if you start talking and identifying that I come from here or there, then there's division, isn't there?

Let's dig deeper even though I'm probably going to get a cryptic response on the next question that stems off this. But primarily they are here. And when we think about the fact, like I've been trying to say when you look at the variations in human types, they are just unbelievably different. There are so many diverse genes in this equation. Clearly, they came from all over the Cosmos to live with us. They shared their genes and that's inside us now.

So now I'm going to talk about the no-forehead beings I've seen, and I have the bones of one individual. Where did these bones come from? What were their intentions?

Mezreth:

Some think it's creation. Some think it's intelligence. Some think it's destruction and some think it's essence. All correct and all are Akashi. We are all garments of Akashi. Life has always been here.

Mixing and merging here, there and everywhere. We've been together for a long time, so long that the idea of ours and yours has lost meaning. We have lost meaning. There are ancient human remains dotted around the cosmos posing equal mysteries. You and they, and we – ours, yours and theirs, all meaningless – all is the same. Origin is the same for all beings.

They were our siblings. Our younger kin. They left the cradle, their home, to travel for the love of curiosity. Then they made friends on and on they would go, but after ages, friendships broken and alliances took over, our little siblings got too involved and lost heart after some time, they abandoned their goals and returned home, never wanting to return again and never wanting to leave again.

Steve:

While we're going down this path, I wanted to try something fairly pragmatic. The last question got close, so we'll try again. We're talking about different races of aliens. And really, it's funny that on this planet, nearly all the talk, apart from Pleiadians and Sirians, seems to be fixated on two groups.

And for a lot of different reasons, which we won't go into right now, I'm not sure that it's completely right, I was wondering if we could have a little bit of detail on the prime suspects in this group, which would probably be the Reptilians and Draconians. What is their take on these two groups, what they're on about and with the current state of play with them. And the consensus is they are in league with the devil and that they're completely evil. But I'm not sure that's right. But let's find out what you got for me.

My thinking is this at the moment the world has never been more preoccupied and possessed with fear. And it basically sucks the life out of people. And I know many people who are just falling underneath it because it's insidious in its grip. It's now become every part of our thinking. People are judged by issues around the damage and grief fear creates, and it's turning people against people.

I would really appreciate a practical response and I don't know what the answer is going to be, but anyway, we're going to try anyway. What is your response to my plea for something?

Mezreth:

We represent only some of the factions. Your closest neighbours, the Xannians, they see, they fear you as you are now. But the needs on why they choose to risk themselves may frighten you in the beginning in essence, their motivations on befriending you are of survival, but you would gain much from that relationship should you master your fear. All they want is an exchange.

This time. This will defeat you, but you will not die. When these days pass, you will marvel at a strength you never knew you had then and only then will you know. You will know those days were a gift.

Transcript Four
Chapter 15

Steve:

I asked about the beginning of life from the Big Bang then everything that followed after, to which he said, life has always been here. Maybe the Big Bang is no more than life creating matter as a place of residence to give purpose and a way to test and measure each soul's progress.

All right. So that's what matter is for, it's a way of creating challenges. And, of course, with every challenge, there's an option within that. On a slightly different tangent I asked Mezreth about God, after all God is the sole agent involved in bringing the Big Bang into existence. He said it was regarded differently in different manifestations, pure equality, intelligence and of course with human features in some cases.

Taking one step backward what of the supposed opposite force to God? There has always been a manifestation in the opposite side to this Divine equation which has often been referred to as Satan or Lucifer. So, the question of what is or was Lucifer is ever-present. I wanted to ask about this.

Is this an opposing energy or force? And, has Lucifer always existed, or is it a collective figment of some people's imagination? And what about this notion of the fallen angel? Is that Lucifer's fate? So, I want to get my head around what is this being that's supposed to be the Supreme Lord of Evil? What's he got to say in that regard?

Mezreth:

The Big Bang was a point of change, but life existed before. Like the many other cataclysms before, when life decided to change. We can still see the waves of the big bang rippling out in the black and its many predecessors. Life changes. It's a must for the universal stagnates and its consciousness falters. Don't fear death of life as you know it. Fear the death of challenge.

You figure it out. Akashi is God, Akashi is Lucifer. Akashi is the same across. It's me and you. Akashi is pull and push inside and outside. Akashi is stupid and intellectual as it is war and peace. There's no opposite to The All as there is no name for non-existence.

Steve:

Well, then the next question becomes superfluous to an extent, but we'll go with it anyway because it'll probably turn into something unexpected. Now, is this force or being Lucifer, purely evil without compassion, or perhaps it is a guardian who's ordained to test and assess the merit and fortitude of each incarnated soul? In asking this I sort of know the answer because he told us before that they're both the same side of us.

Question number four, a question where I think I already know the answer. Back to our Creator and the designs and tests. There are three beliefs on this planet in regard to what happens when the body dies, nothing at all, we spend eternity after one life in the immortal plane of Heaven or Hell or reincarnating since the beginning. But only one of them can be right. I feel like this is going to be very straightforward, an easy answer to predict-which is a very rare event when talking to Mezreth. Then the question is which of the three options is right?

All I can get is a basic take on this. Sounds to me like each soul chooses, if you believe nothing you get nothing, so too if convinced it is just one life on-world, so be it. But if you either believe in, or embrace once knowing it is your call, that reincarnation is the way to go, then that's where you go, again and again. Outside that thumbnail sketch I'm just going to pass on adding more. Lea made a comment that deeply resonated with me in relation to the inner battle being a constant issue for every soul breathing. Whereas she said some try to manage their demons while others hide them, and that those who deceive themselves must bear the consequences.

Mezreth:

We are flawed because there would be no other reason to continue. Distractions are also a test for you given by you. The ones who fall behind, who do damage are children. Nothing more or less. They should not be praised or pitied. You know how long that path will be. And it will take many years or lifetimes for them to see but wish them well on the journey that all of us had to take.

Justice. If you want to master content, you will. If you wish, splendour and joy, you will. If you wish damnation because you feel deserved, you will. If you wish to return to the canvas, you will not.

Management of demon thoughts are here for that. Again, management of demons is the key to unlock the higher doors of existence. Sometimes it's tricky to figure out which ones need management, since they shapeshift into other issues that need attention. Sadly, the ones that cause the most grief and shame is why so few are willing to face them. But remember, those feelings are their way of deterring you from your self-mastery.

Steve:

I wanted to go further here in asking, what are demons? And their opposites, are they angels? Or, are these angels Aliens, or are they mystical beings of an ethereal constitution? What are these things/entities within he talked about?

Now I want to personalise this journey into the stars and the beginning in asking a question that relates to him alone. Do you regret coming or being posted here? Because I don't know which it is, to be honest. And where is your home planet?

Remaining on this theme of present residence irrespective of whether it's everywhere or one locality. I wanted to find out if what many claim, including Lea, is true. Where there times in the past when aliens and humans lived together on this planet? And if so, why did this arrangement stop?

During these times of chaos, suspicion and fear why didn't some of the aliens who were not subjected to this imbalance come down and offer assistance or guidance. Why didn't they come down and say boys and girls this is what we should do?

Now let's look deeper into the psyche of these earthly inhabitants only this time instead of probing into our faults and deficiencies, what of the positives? What quality do humans have that you find most appealing and inspiring, and what qualities do they also possess that you find most disappointing?

Mezreth:

Demons and angels are figments of your mind's way of trying to understand itself. Such as untold scores of souls, figments of Akashi trying to understand itself. If you speak intent, they are intangible terms. Our presence has been thoroughly documented there and you assume that's to certain roles long before you understood who we are.

I was born in vacuum. You were born on stone. Where the vacuum and stone is not relevant. Since we are born here in this universe, I have no regrets in my coming here, but I'm not void of regrets.

In times of Atlantis, we were together, and even before that. All peoples in the interstellar community were too young to appreciate each other. So, they returned to their cradles to grow a little more. Lots of lanterns. I was already lost for the moon guardians lost themselves.

We are. We're doing it now, as we've always done. We won't burst into the bedroom while a child wields a gun. It's a recipe for further heartache. I've seen the consequences before. If you want us to do more, you must reach us halfway.

Humans create innovative ways to cheat the test.

Steve:

I've got one more question left to ask and to me in some respects, this is the one we're focused on the most. Ten years from now, could you briefly, briefly describe what that would look like on the planet Earth and those humans allowed to remain?

It's written in a lot of scriptures, that there will be a golden age of a thousand years where everything's perfect. And I've seen Christian literature and depictions where you've got people sitting down with a lamb and a lion and they're all patting one another.

That's not going to happen. We're not going to have a thousand years of golden evil-free existence where everyone smiles at each other, and no-one is challenged or called to task. But I suppose when you think about it, there's not one person on this planet that's perfect. There'll be a mixture of people with different strengths and weaknesses, and some people will still not like other people. There still will be things said about other people they won't like. If that didn't happen, if there was nothing that was disruptive or upsetting, then there would be nothing for us to learn.

Mezreth:

A new set of problems but you won't be able to solve them without moulding the tools from your current issues. Don't worry about tomorrow.

We are flawed because there would be no reason to continue this.

Transcript Five
Chapter 16

Steve:

I wanted to focus on one theory, one aspect, which is the existence of Heaven and Hell. Why? Because it's the focal issue of concern for every being on this planet that dies. If we understood why we are here and what happens after the physical body dies, this life would be a lot easier. So, let's have a go. No guarantee we'll get any right answers.

The first question I wrote is related to the popular notion of hell is a lack of a location. But is that true? After completing a ceremony recently with one of the rings from Atlantis, and I'm not going to go into the details, there are two lines from a song that resonated with me. By the way, I don't have any INXS albums.

There is one song that has the words, 'the devil inside, the devil inside, every single one of us has the devil inside." Is the lyricist, right? So that's the first question. If so, how do we deal with this demon in residence? Is it best to fight, flight or manage?

When people talk about the fact that you go up to heaven and down for hell, that's their internal location. It's all in here, isn't it? So, the INXS quote is valid, which it obviously is, so does the reverse reply in relation to what is termed Heaven? We sort of answered this before, but any clarification or extension will assist. Other people who have died return describing different scenes and setting. Is that a place of internal construct or actual location.

Mezreth:

Heaven and hell are not separate planes, nor are they on Earth. They live within you. You're your own angels and demons. Any good or misfortune that befalls you is sometimes out of one's control. But what is your ability to handle it. If you run from your demons, they grow larger. If you fight them, then you become them. But if you master yourself, then you are king.

What you experience in your afterlife, is only for you to know. I don't know for certain what you'll see and feel, but if you know you're alive, then you will know more than I.

Steve:

When this topic was last raised, Mezreth spoke of one supreme entity, there was no division. If so, what is Lucifer or Satan? Is this purely an internal manifestation or an interlocutor and manager of negative energies and co-author of the exam you spoke of that humans can't creatively avoid or suspend? My question is, what is this concept that we have of Lucifer and Satan? Is it our own head creating it, or is there a spirit of some form that is an organizer?

With the devil given its rightful position that brings us back to the exam Mezreth said we so cleverly avoid, of which humans found excuses and distractions. In a nutshell, what is the content and curriculum of this exam?

What is this exam that we are so cleverly able to avoid?

Let's look outside ourselves and take some time to consider another factor in the Alien equation of which there are so many to choose from. Was there ever a species of reptilians living on this planet either before or during the time of hominids? It is a constant topic of conversation and I feel some clarity is needed here. Do these reviled reptilians actually exist? And if so, what was and maybe still is, their general opinion of Homo sapiens?

Mezreth:

Lucifer is a symbol, a category for you to better understand the fluidity of existence. Like all other divine entities, they are representatives of virtues for you to choose, to adapt or discard. The power of choice is frightening, but it is your fundamental right.

You make the right choice. The exam is to see if you are going to make the right choice. Every one of those choices are bought with consequences. You've always been at the crossroads, but now those crossroads cannot be ignored or left until later. Apathy won't save you.

There's been many species on and around earth, like many other worlds. It's not unique. There's a long history with humans and Zanashj, but Zanashj are not reptilian, though their appearance can trick the inexperienced eye. They were shapeshifters taking faces of many to adapt to many environments. They made poor choices, but now seek redemption from those they have damaged. Some are here now, learning from the same school as you.

Steve:

They sort of do fit into that reptilian mould that we've given them, but we've done that basically because we've looked at them like I did. I can superficially see the reptilian side in there. That's just their physical features and that means very little.

I'm looking at the next question and I sort of asked this before, but I'll read it out, because I was really trying to chase this up from so many different angles. Some have theorized the inspiration behind the concept of the devil incarnate on this planet is a reptilian leader spirit full and vengeance. Is the concept of a devil a fictional account used to make the flock fearful?

You're referring to. Who, us?

We got a lot of exactly what we were looking for. We are our demons and devils, and they are us.

With Lucifer being a human construct and excuse, we do need to examine our motives and intentions. The human condition is an enigmatic and contradictory piece of work. All nonhuman, earthly species seem to have a general set of ways of behaving and interacting. Humans can be serial killers, philosophers, pacifists and mercenaries. We can be Hitler, Stalin, Tesla, Ghandi, Plato and Martin Luther King.

Why are we so unpredictable because all other animals on this planet have general traits of behaviour, and they are fairly predictable. You cannot predict any human on this planet, why is that?

Mezreth:

Stories change and shift from the bias, from the biased mouths of the teller and the biased ears of the listener, those that are not physically repulsive if they do not wish it so. Their actions, however, were so they were depicted as such. Those that were never pure evil. If evil did have a face, it would be one of beauty and innocence. You and they have a lot in common. You and they have a lot of common ground.

Yes. Collectively.

The human condition is not exclusive to humans. No one will ever be free from it. The difference is we devoted more time to communication and understanding of each individual, what their strengths and weaknesses are. We know why someone is the way they are. We know why they have made their choices. And we try to facilitate environments where they flourish. They are like seeds, but no two seeds are alike.

Steve:

Mezreth did say that we are at the crossroads at this time, and that we've got to make a decision. So it does follow from that question. Why is it so important right now for each person to choose? Is it to balance their books, make amends and control their demons; is that because there is an exam ahead that no one can cheat or avoid? And if so, what is the mark if you have score to earn the right to stay?

You've got to own up to your sins and indiscretions too. That might be hard for some people, knowing that this interaction has been going on for so long with so many different alien species involved, has there ever been conflict or serious disagreement between them? And if so, how has this been resolved? And having you telling me that they're no different to us, I have to assume that they must have had conflict. How did they get around that?

Since we found the three rings, they have been associated with chaos, deceit, lies, sickness, curses and murder ceremonies. It's a situation they thrive in, but are the rings solely responsible due to their evil disposition? Or do they merely shake free the devil inside. Are the three rings from Atlantis a conduit that seeks out and amplifies your demons, or is there something more sinister contained within each ring?

Mezreth:

If you have correctly nurtured a person, you have saved the world. The exam is your life, and the results are the lives that come after. The only failure is the one where you repeat the same mistakes in the assumption that you will pass. For now, the passing grade is to avoid making that same mistake in this century.

The Zanashj have been humbled by their arrogance, their assumption that they sat at the top of the pyramid in their sphere of influence, made them forgetful and small. Their weaknesses were discovered and exploited, and the dominion on many worlds shrunk until their influence caved in. Earth was also in their dominion, but you (humans,) you cast them away at the right time. Zanashj have never recovered from those days, nor do they ever intend on repeating them. Can you say the same for yourselves?

They're only tools. They maximize whatever traits you have, and your ego becomes larger from their monstrous power, and they will only add to that vicious cycle. Those tools are also part of the exam, and the right choice is to leave them be. Atlanteans had similar tools that allowed their empire to flourish and look what happened.

Transcript Six
Chapter 17

Steve:

Duncan Roads told me of a time when his pet dog was on death's door, he contacted the best animal whisperer in the country for guidance. She began by asking him to leave the room as he was the problem. And I can tell you, Duncan was shocked because he loves that dog.

When he was allowed to return, she told him that because Duncan was trying so hard to keep the dog alive and with him, the dog couldn't cross over and was solely hanging on for him. She said the dog had a secret, and this is where it gets interesting. His dog had a sacred role on the other side in teaching dogs how to control their more basic instincts and devote themselves to teaching humans unconditional love. Was he correct?

What follows is whether this is just dogs, or does this extend further, and if so, how far? On this occasion I was inspired by Lea and it's to do with our last conference. And what people didn't see before we started, was that Lea had a cat crawling all over her. Now the cat clearly loved and cared about her. Could it be that some cats have also been given the task of teaching humans pure love?

Mezreth:

Animals are not masters or servants to any other animal, but two souls can arrange their roles for each other.

Cats and dogs express love differently from physical to a soul level, same as some humans and non-terrestrials. My expression of love is unlike to the kin beside me. What matters is that expression.

Steve:

I want to close this animal connection with a personal anecdote and musing that relates to Mezreth's insistence that the soul of any animal is no different than ours. Evans rabbit lived over thirteen years, which is exceptionally long for any rabbit. We would like to think that when we pass over, his soul will greet us. Is that just wishful thinking or the real truth?

What I find fascinating is that the animals also get to choose according to what they want, that is no different to us and makes me wonder what is the difference between humans and many sorts of life? The last three questions lead into the question I really wanted to ask, and that's why I went about this in steps. The question I find really interesting and I'm not sure how this is going to turn out, sums up the other three. Speaking of souls, is there any difference at all between dogs, cats and rabbits, and that of humans?

Many assume that birds communicate solely by sound, but I've got an issue with that. How can flocks of hundreds and sometimes thousands of bird's twist and turn while in flight all at the same time in perfect synchronicity, yet never collide. You put a mob of humans clustered together and see what happens, and they'll trample and collide.

Obviously, something's going on there. What am I looking at there? What happens with these birds? Is this all through one bird's audible or visual direction, or are all birds communicating through some form of communal telepathic thought process that we don't fully understand yet?

Mezreth:

When souls depart life, they shed parts of the former personality, which is is copied over, but what they were in life was returned to something more balanced. Some souls wish to wait. What some souls wish is to find other fields. But if there was a strong bond to the living, then they often say I can't.

No difference. There's no cats, no snakes, no human soul – it's totally pure. Those former states are gone, except, the only difference is the wisdom and experience gained to aid in the advancement of that self.

The living and dead ride the waves of the sea of consciousness. We all feel it, but not all know it. It's part of the invisible orchestra of the universe. In some places, the music is mute, while in other places, the music is full. Earth has a song, but it's a pity only few can hear it.

Steve:

Let's stay with the birds a little further and talk about those wild birds that are flying all over the place. If flying free, that cannot include the chooks and birds we put in cages because that kills their lifestyle, vitality and changes so many things.

Exclude the domesticated birds which do not count. I'm talking about the birds in the rainforest where we live at the moment that fly as they wish and go where they want.

We've got these birds circling freely in the sky, of which there are billions of birds on this planet at any given time. And most birds, except the parrots, don't live that long so I've got an issue with the death-count. Now this is where it gets tricky, if not killed by a predator, climatic extreme, collision or speeding cars, I've never seen a dead bird. I've been out in the bush a lot, more than most people and not once have I seen a dead bird laying anywhere.

What I've seen are thousands flying around. Now, this is an issue for me. Why aren't we knee-deep in feathers? How do these birds die and where are the bodies, because I can't find them, and I have been looking for clues or feathered corpses.

You hear them all the time, but they're never on the ground. I want to know where they go when they die because I'm not finding them anywhere. This is a different type of question, and for the first time I am not sure you can answer it, but it's one that's puzzled me for quite some time now.

Mezreth:

The world is a large place. It moves, even the invisible walls shift on the rock and water. For every one known place in this world, there are a thousand hidden places, right?

Steve:

We're beginning to realize that trees communicate and interact with each other. My question is, can that interaction extend further than just within themselves?

That's where I want to go. And in particular, I want to look at one form of that communication, which is quite radical. And I want to see how we get a reaction to that. We've been told by two psychics that the ancient no forehead skull, which we are custodians of, that it was called a long time ago to this planet.

Now, this is where it gets difficult even for me still to this day. But it wasn't called by hominids and not even by what we mistakenly call Reptilians. It was the trees, this is what I was told twice. That the trees called these aliens to this planet because it was being devastated, it was being destroyed, the trees were being attacked, war and pollution was rife, and the trees collectively called them to help. Is that possible? And if it is, how did the trees communicate with beings on the other side of the cosmos? Because that is a huge leap in everything, even for me.

The rocks we have are aware and they have both energy and magic. We're aware of that. And a lot of the people we're talking to are also equally aware of that. The question I've got is, that awareness, energy and magic we have experienced, is that force in them which has been there from the beginning or through the actions and ceremonies of humans, or is it somewhere in between?

Mezreth:

One tree is simple. Pulled apart molecule by molecule, the lifeform is almost mechanical. Just like a single neuron. However, only when you bundle them, a connection forms, information is exchanged and assimilated to the point where they begin to change themselves in the universal world around them. That one tree is so much more than it was before. It is part of a web and the stronger the web, the greater their song.

Life is not restricted to just biological lifeforms. There is far more life out there than you believe. Life existed here long before organic life grew. Everything is affected by something, and that energy embeds itself into anything close with enough years of energy. A simple pebble can hold enough information to summon a soul and a song.

Steve:

In other words, a piece of rock can become a receptacle. All the people that touch it, they can make a deposit or withdrawal if the rock is willing and person in congress with the rock is worthy. So, we have killing rocks that have been used to kill, rocks that can heal humans and rocks that can enlighten, each sacred rock we have has a role to play in the affairs of people. In concluding this session, I want to leave the rocks for now and return to us. First up, is there any distinguishing feature or ability humans have that separates us from all other earthly lifeforms?

What has been lost in translation is that we are all animals, not just sapiens, but all hominids are part of one family. And that truth leads on to the question as to why one strand out of at least sixteen hominids prevailed, all others mysteriously became extinct at around about 12,000 years ago? We know that the Neanderthals, the Denisovans and so many others all disappeared at around that time. Let's be honest, and I've said this often, we were not the smartest of the sixteen 'kids on the block', not by a long shot. In fact, my latest calculations based on skull sizes ranks us at number six. There are no less than five hominids in front of us. And most probably when they find more, we will slip further down the pecking order. The scientists will tell you these ridiculous stories that we were smarter the Neanderthals and Denisovans, and they know that is clearly untrue. Their skulls are bigger. This is a very important question. Why is it we survived, and they didn't? Is it simply because our genetic strand was the most pliable and accommodating for alien species to mould and manipulate? Or is it something else?

Mezreth:

The belief that humans are singular is the only difference. Arrogant ignorance is what makes you distinguished.

The others aren't extinct. They have biologically survived into the soup of humanity. Cast away the illusion of uniqueness. There are many worlds who consider themselves to be the only ones like them. Each one of them, like humanity, are a blend and are surviving. They and you are living dreams of ancient genius. You assume you are a singular thing, but you already were many things long before you became humans. We were all born to different stars. But each of us came from the same place.

Transcript Seven
Chapter 18

Steve:

Question number one stems out of an article I read in Duncan Road's magazine, Nexus. It was an interview, I think, with a lady called Linda Mall or something like that. And it was a question-and-answer session with one alien. And it went like this. One area of discussion related to how aliens genetically modified humans.

Now I have no issue with that concept, but in Australia, as opposed to elsewhere, I've always been of the opinion it was a partnership by consent and was steeped in equality. And this is where this gets a bit tricky for me. Basically, the premise was they took a very crude and less intelligent hominid to see whether it could be bred up to be more intelligent and aware. Is it as simple as this or there are nuances not raised?

There are suggestions, some incredibly convoluted trying to explain why this happened. Some claim our chins were responsible for our continuation, another suggestion is that our fat cells have given us that extra advantage. So, the big question is why is it all the other hominids aren't here, but we are. What happened to them?

Mezreth:

That's true, but there have been a few that have altered your development. Our original model, what my kin had intended for you, was different from what you are now. You have also been touched by the Zanashj and those that live outside.

The other types have never become extinct. They survived in modern humans. Your biological tools allowed you to prevail many changes, and they were given to you by nature and by us. Remember, we blended ingredients, but nature incubated.

Steve:

I have commented on this general proposition already, but said nothing about the last sentence, that is a new extension worthy of further reflection and serious consideration. Frederic Slater stated in his reading of the Buragurra engravings that man was brought to Earth then placed in a "deep sleep from which they were awakened in the prime of life. They found themselves surrounded by glorious game abounding ..." What happened during that time of stasis and how long it lasted is unknown, but there is a considerable gap and that is in complete accord with what Mezreth knows to be true. How this came to pass is still unknown, but what is less debatable is that if you look at the different ancient artifacts, Dreaming stories, paintings and archaeology in Australia, there were earlier times when aliens and humans lived on Earth together and we've made that clear before.

If so, when and why did that cohabitation cease?

Clearly warnings were given. Lea, I do remember you saying when you talked about this on earlier occasions, you did say there were aliens living in Atlantis. And just before the change when Atlantis lost its way and the crystals blew up, they just left without fanfare or fuss in the years before. They didn't really give any explanation as to why they were going. They just quietly absconded. Will there be a time in the foreseeable future when the Aliens will return to this planet and live with us again?

It would seem Earth has hosted many types of beings, some originate from here, while others do not. The other beings born here, what do they actually look like? What did they look like? And how do they regard us?

Mezreth:

This was a time of Atlantis when that separation really began this issue. In Atlantia, we lived together here and now there as the culture changed. So did the hearts and minds, paranoia and pride eat away at the Atlanteans. They wanted to be stars. Warnings were given but the stars closed their eyes and then they remained closed.

We want to share this interstellar community with you once again. But we need assurances you will open your eyes. If you cannot then you cannot, then it will only be you who suffers.

Earth has been a home to many beings. Some have been transient and were born there. They have left in crafts and others walked away from the world. You will reunite them again. They wait by the shining dog Sirius.

Steve:

Oh, hence the connection to Sirius. Egyptians were obsessed by Sirius. The ones who live on Sirius, are they the most human-like in appearance? I suppose his reply hints at a yes.

During the long period of time when sapiens lived along so many of the different types of hominids, the portrayal is that we actually wiped them all out because we were better at stabbing people, being devious and violent. That's what we're being told. Was it a peaceful or warlike existence between these different hominids? If there were mainly times of conflict, where were the sapiens positioned in the fighting pecking order?

Now let's talk about the soul Mezreth never leaves alone, and the journey it takes when separating from the body. I know the ancient Egyptians, Original people and Gnostics have a belief that upon death, the soul splits into three. One portion is purely physical, which ceases to exist upon death. But, of the other two parts, half goes into a place of rest, reflection, and perhaps reincarnates. And we come back yet again, if we choose to.

That destination of refection and accountability most people will accept, some people call it Heaven, Bliss or Nirvana, it doesn't really matter about names or titles. Now this is where it gets complicated, as the other half goes back in the country, a sacred site or even bones, and if not, it returns into what Yung refers to as the collective unconscious. Is that belief true or false?

Mezreth:

Conflict is what drives a soul to change. For better or worse, there was conflict, but there was also peace. However, when these groups fell in love with their greatness, the conflicts turned to wars, and any semblance of peace was the first to become extinct.

The soul departs to a place for reflection. The body returns to the land so that the soul may have a chance to live again. Today you are breaking that cycle.

Steve:

In making the right choice it seems to me we are inherently handicapped, as our experts assure us that we use up the 15% of the brain and the rest does nothing beyond spectating, and they also claim the same ratio applies to our genes. And it has always been like this. Basically, if I was to compare that illogical diagnosis to a car, you got one and a quarter cylinder working and six and three quarters marking time. Has that always been the case or is this just something that has occurred in recent times?

Mezreth:

Yes, but you can learn how to use more parts. You have the potential for psionics. However, with the right training and manifesting, many more doors will fly open so and actually there is a further answer.

Steve:

The best way to do something, especially with the children, because as we know they still have parts of those areas of their brain that are more mystical and magical ready and willing if engaged, is encourage children to seek out visions and stay in contact with their 'imaginary friends.' As a counter the experts and adults must convince that what the child sees and hears from across the divide is not there. It didn't happen, it's a make-believe friend. We've all heard that one. And so many children get told they're looking at and hearing their imagination or themselves. And what we to do is make sure that we totally repress the psychic talents at the start of a child's life, and it is only when that is done and dusted they're ready to live in the adult 'real world'.

Strangely enough this etheric theme was originally a central part of language and that is especially so when dealing with the first language spoken. We often make mention of the Original First Language that was spoken around the world in ancient times. And if people don't believe that there was one global language in ancient times, we suggest you go to the Bible. There is extensive talk about the Tower of Babylon. When there was a time when everyone could speak one language, and then they didn't.

Is that a metaphor, or is it a literal statement of a truth?

Well, my question is, was there a First Language spoken around the planet?

Mezreth:

The first language is thought, understanding oneself and one's surroundings to communicate these concepts beyond telepathy is beholden to thought like mathematics is beholden to logic, the desire to understand one surroundings. The first language is the tongue of the soul.

Transcript Eight
Chapter 19

Steve:

I want to start this session with three quotes from Edgar Cayce and hopefully responses from you as to whether he was right or wrong and why. First up, Cayce did originally think that astrology was bogus and of no substance. And to be honest, up until quite recently, I was inclined to think the same way or give it very little serious consideration. That's changed. Cayce was shocked by two things that were in his readings while sleeping, the word reincarnation, and the other offending utterance was astrology, because he was a devout Christian, those things just don't belong.

And he had a lot of issues dealing with his content. But this is what he actually said. This is what the sleeping prophet kept returning to. During these sessions that spanned across so many curtains he told those in attendance that the stars represent soul patterns. The twelve signs of the Zodiac are twelve patterns, from which the soul chooses when coming onto the earth. They relate to races, patterns of temperament, personality, etc. Is he correct?

Mezreth:

Don't worry. He is not right in his conclusions. But you must remember the outer universe is a reflection of the inner universe. And if the heart bends, the hand follows. The universe moves in spite for you, in love for you, and always around you.

Steve:

Cayce claimed that in every 2160 years, a different age of the Zodiac is in position that dominates the earth. It goes backward and therefore is called a precession. During the heyday of Egypt, the sign of Taurus the bull was in the commanding position. So the people of Egypt worshipped the bull. And that's really got me, as it were, it was an overt sign. The sun was actually in Scorpio and was shining across Taurus. He's saying that influence is global, maybe even cosmic, as opposed to just personal.

This reminds me of a scene in a show called Friends where the girl with the blond hair, Phoebe, is talking to Joey. She was patting Joey on the head, consoling him because he said he couldn't remember anything about his past lives. And she said, "well, that's no surprise" because "you're a brand-new soul." I thought that line was mildly amusing at the time.

I did give some credence to this comment. We often hear this comment passed on to someone who is not aware or insightful, as being a young soul. However, Cayce says that all of the souls God created came into existence at the very beginning, and none have been made since. It seems everything is timeless, was Cayce right or wrong to say that all souls were made at the beginning?

Mezreth:

The only universe that we have any semblance of control over is the one on the inside. And if you can master that, then the rest follows.

Our souls are broken and forged, absorbed and separated at all times. There is no beginning. And there is no end. The only time is a circle of eternity. A piece of stone, as it is, may be a mere eon, but the energy of the stone is timeless. Just as my soul may be an eon, the age of my energy is forever.

Steve:

That's actually a stunning answer, if "the energy of a stone is timeless," that must also apply to the souls of everything. It seems that this time Cayce was correct.

With the soul created at the beginning, I wanted to return to the nature and duality of the soul, in particular what the ancient Egyptians, Gnostics, and Original Dreaming and now Cayce reluctantly also stated. Now, he didn't say it specifically because he's a Christian, but in the end of one sleeping session he talked about the soul. He spoke about being broken into two separate parts. But it's very specific. He was saying what I said. That one half of the soul moved beyond the curtain to reflect and consider will it most likely be reincarnated in the future, while the other half stayed behind going into the country or what Jung would call the collective unconscious. Bearing in mind Mezreth did say that souls are broken, reforged, split up and moved around.

Within all that movement and separation, it reunites with the other half when it returns to take on a new life on this planet. Is this correct?

Mezreth:

Upon death, an explosion of consciousness happens. It pours into everything, and everyone who is around the deceased, it partially embeds itself into the relative material world around it, but the surviving soul, it departs if chooses to do so. Some choose to linger and bond with their old world. Some are lost and others wander.

Steve:

I'm not sure whether Mezreth is agreeing with an actual division as such, but I'm going to take that as close to yes. Irrespective of how the soul is constituted when we incarnate in on this planet, we lose most to nearly all of our awareness and knowledge of heaven or nirvana while in bodily form. I've been told by Lea, that Mezreth has incarnated in bodily form. When he did this, when he came to this planet, did the same rules apply? Did he lose the big picture knowledge, which is what that is? Or did he retain all of it, or somewhere in between?

And if he did, how is this possible? Because I thought that there is a rule that when you came here, you had to be tested by being prompted into a leap of faith. So, the question is, what state of awareness did he bring across with him?

Mezreth:

It doesn't matter what new life a soul reincarnates into. They will never be able to remember every memory of their past lives. However, one must be open to the memories peeking through, not shying away. No matter how heartbreaking the memory, the more you pull away, the less your current mind will be able to remember. There are many reasons why someone cannot recall their past lives. They refuse to do so. They don't understand what they are.

And for others, they have a thick haze wrapped around their souls that stops them. My old life, I viewed the world through a keyhole. I was ignorant by accident and arrogant by choice. I made many mistakes for my soul to learn from. But those mistakes are being paid by others. That's why I'm here. My perspective was narrow then, so it may be wider now.

Steve:

Basically, while incarnated here, you don't know anything about the other side. Therefore, everything you do is either a leap of faith or a leap of the wrong way.

Mezreth for reasons I am sure he will or may reveal in the future, has shared details of some of my past-lives. But not only the outlines but specifics and inner motivations were spoken of. I actually thought, and told this to Lea often, that knowing so much of her past was an incredible burden to bear, never expecting I was soon to go through the same process. What did throw me was that he knew of my actions and intentions, which I'm not going to talk about because that's not really on point. All of this leads up to a question that has been ever-present how is it possible to create such an intimate contact while he is existing somewhere completely differently from where I am at that particular moment in time? How can you do that? How can you actually read other people like that and know what they've done?

I'd like to once again make this personal in trying to analyse a form or manner of existence to Mezreth, is your existence in a spiritual or mortal form? Lea has told me you're both, which in itself is difficult to comprehend, but there is some form of flesh and bone in your equation.

So, if he inhibits a mortal body I would assume his body, like ours, dies. And if doesn't, why not? And secondly, what is his major form of existence?

Mezreth:

Souls move together in each life, like a herd. We know each other now because we knew each other before. Each of us were friends, lovers and enemies. The phenomena of eternity.

From the beginning, my kin can do both. Some choose permanence of one. We all age, but only a few of us have chosen to die. Be grateful for your brief lives, for you can transcend faster and experience divinity sooner.

Steve:

That's amazing. So, they don't know what their life expectancy is because most have never reached it, for them death never happened unless they forced the issue. Would that explain why there are a lot of myths eulogising what many claim to be the fountain of youth. This quest that enables humans to live forever, coupled with medical experts claiming that aging is a disease, not a process itself, opens up all sorts of possibilities.

Either way, whether dying or never dying while deposited on this same mortal plane, there are three things that came to mind. Does he eat, does he sleep, and can he experience pain?

I'm still stuck on the phrase "if we chose to". For us it is not a choice but compulsory, for his kind it is the ultimate extension of the oft heard mantra of freedom of choice. Now we have dispensed with the physical side of Mezreth's existence, and am none the wiser, I would like to talk about what Mezreth's main focus and possible reason he chose not to die as some of his kind preferred. Are there some earthly incarnated souls that you take more interest in? Because there's quite a few on the planet right now. There's around seven billion plus of them. And I can't imagine that he's taking personal interest in all seven billion, because that would do your head in. What is it about the souls you chose to work with that makes it worth the effort?

What advice would you give all human beings during these turbulent times right now? What advice would you give knowing that my understanding is that things are running to a conclusion. Has he got any advice or gems of wisdom he can pass on so we can pass this on to others?

Mezreth:

Of course. Well, without pain, we cannot know joy or boundaries. We eat and sleep if we choose to do so.

There have been many because they remind us of ourselves, of where we were, where we are now, and where we want to be, all things.

Don't lie to yourselves.

Transcript Nine
Chapter 20

Steve:

I remember before you mentioned Elzona is a planet that has incredible music and art on it – according to you it is better than here. My question to Mezreth is why is there such a unique artistic dynamic on earth? In music, you have rock, jazz, country, rap, etc. and so many different people like so many different genres. The same diversity and taste exist in art also. Is this kind of diversity unique on earth?

Well, that is a bit disappointing as I had us in first place throughout the Universe. My thinking was the art and music was what Mezreth's mob were so attracted to, turns out we are second best or even worse. It seems to me if we want to catch up and narrow the gap, we have to dump our addiction to destroying. From my biased point of view, I'd like to add to that lightening of the musical garbage in banning disco, rap and quite a lot of country and western music. This really is one massive cosmic laboratory, an experiment with a rock and water petri dish, but it's cosmic, not earthly. That's the interesting part of this. On this planet we've got millions of organisms, seven billion different faces, so many types of geology, geography, and vegetation, everything is so massively varied. There's so much that's going on. And my question is, is this countless diversity the cosmic norm or exception?

Mezreth:

Elzona is a world even my kin question why we decided to add our children on its face. That world's secrets lay deeper than her core. It is a very strange world, there are far more mysteries there than on earth. Ezoni (the guardians of Elzona, much like humans are guardians of earth) have unmatched diversity in their art and much of their inspiration comes of the dynamic, wonderful and terrifying mysteries of their beloved world: Elzona. Why do they create so much? Because they can create, whereas humans gave themselves permission to destroy.

The only extremes on Earth are the psychological, you live in a cooking pot of dangerous and beautiful. These extremes breed extremes. However, don't mistake this as a negative it is essential for you to find the balance within yourselves and understand the why. Only then you can understand us.

Steve:

What Mezreth is agreeing to is that this is a melting pot of extremes, not just on a genetic and physical level, but this is merely a reflection of what lays beneath and what's inside. Of recent there is one extremity that has really ramped up, which is fear and violence. And if you think about it, the ways that we've killed other people, the different techniques and weapons used is almost unbelievable. It used to be a long time back a spear, knife or blade was the sum total on hand.

I read an article in Nexus featuring an interview with an alien who made the claim that trees are very rare in the in this universe. Equally, there are reports and rumours maintaining that the trees on this planet were once miles high. Is this true?

Let's leave the distress of the trees and return to the cause of their grief, humans. Dolores Canon said that the timing of incarnation into a foetus baby is not that specific. She said that the soul might occupy the newly growing body from the point of conception up until the time it is taking its first breath, which means this could happen once the baby leaves the mother.

Cayce was a devout Christian and had a real issue, with the content he supplied while asleep. Who was in contact with Cayce? Was it God, an angel, a spirit or one of your mob?

Mezreth:

Trees, like biological life, are technically a cosmic rarity. Only technically because there's no biological life on Mars and Uranus, Jupiter, Pluto, Mercury. It's a majority that don't have biological life. However, on worlds with biological life, trees are not a cosmic rarity in in that scope. It's true that trees on Earth are biologically unique, like on a Elzona, like on Xann and many more.

The trees on Earth were meant to evolve to a greater consciousness biosphere. However, they are sadly, putting in efforts to adapt to modern human meddling to the naked human eye. Trees appear to be mere mechanical organisms, simple and unassuming. However, they can communicate across a whole continent to many different organisms faster, and more effectively than the phone. The biological internet.

It can depend on how quick the soul decides to occupy the foetus. The most common time for soul entering a growing pineal gland in a human host averages for two months. But there are many different organisms with different gestation periods. But this is specifically talking about humans and also depends on how steadfast that soul is to actually occupy.

Some tend to want to linger around until the right time comes around the potential parent and potential body, and then it links in with it.

My kin and I speak to anyone who needs to listen.

Steve:

From that complete state of ignorance in all things Atlantean he then went on to insist that over half the Americans alive had a past life in Atlantis. Is this why there is such a deep fascination with Atlantis? The drawback is that is it advisable to spend so much time trying to rekindle the Atlantean flame, when it is so tainted, while the little known about Lemuria is entirely positive and certainly worth emulating? Could you share with us some of the traits and positives coming out of Lemuria that seem to be lost in translation?

Perhaps one of the defining issues that leads on to chaos and a disconnection with Mother Nature is the vexed issue of over-population. What was the maximum population of Atlantis and Lemuria?

Now, some people give the more advanced angelic beings names like the Archangel Michael along with other titles. In all narratives of angels, they are supposed to live forever. In every account most of them are able to travel long distances quickly, are tall and have humanlike features. Yeah, you can throw wings on some of them, but that might be put there because if I could fly through the air or levitate, depicting wings is symbolically equivalent to having wings.
That description also fits when itemizing the features of yourself, and. your companions. Is that merely a coincidence or is it because you and your kind are the same as angels?

Mezreth:

All modern humans have ties to the golden age of Atlantia. Although not all were Atlanteans. And if Atlantia was the clock and Alkhem was the jewel, then Lemuria was the wand.

Atlantia had tens of millions spanning across the island. Lemuria reached over a million. Lemuria was a place to visit, not to live.

We copied some of our form over to our children. You adopted your own features over time and impressed what you desire into art, as did we. Vanity is not exclusive to humans. You call many beings angels. I have been referred to as an angel, also a fallen one, neither wrong nor right.

Steve:

My last question in this session is based around something Mezreth said earlier which really resonated with me. Is there a passage in any scripture that recommends self-loathing as the path to salvation. To an extent I understand why you said this. But we live in a global society where so many lifestyle coaches implore that we have to love ourselves unconditionally, and because of this, many might find your dictum to hate yourself somewhat puzzling.

Could you explain in more detail why you said this?

Mezreth:

Because this is an essential part to spiritual development because you have to identify the wrongs before you can identify the rights. Unfortunately, on Earth, we do have this predilection for self-loathing and so people tend to listen more to self-criticism over self-love first. Self-love is a vehicle to salvation, but not many understand what self-love truly means. So I speak in ways that express clearer parts of this idea for you: you self-hate when you succumb to lounging an hour longer than you want, you self-hate when you continue a forced smile, you self-hate when you tell yourself you are higher and most righteous than all others. You must resist these small beliefs. Self-love is doing anything you can to live, not survive, even if it takes you to places of pain.

Transcript Ten
Chapter 21

Steve:

Has Australia always been part of Lemuria? Some Original Elders I've spoken to refer to this country as Mu and I've heard others say the same thing. If it is, could you supply a general geographical sketch map of the entire Lemurian continent?

Obviously, Lemuria includes Original people of Australia, which is one group, and then there are also some Asian and Pacific Island people within this confederation. And even though they do have different cultures, somehow all coexisted.

The next question flows off this to an extent and we're probably going to get roughly the same answer. You said previously that it was sparsely populated compared to Atlantis. What was the main settlement pattern? Was it hunter gatherer, small villages or cities with a capped population?

Mezreth:

The freehold of Lemuria stretched from the North Pacific Islands all the way to the shores of Africa. Lemuria was not a city nor a nation. It was a world of its own. Atlantis found their way to the crocodile's nose for many millennia, until they were judged and ultimately expelled.

Modest tribes were scattered. They had nexus meeting points to discuss and exchange. These points were great places for refuge, but none did make them home. It was home to Lemuria and her invisible children, each nexus point was equally spread for each community. There is a reason why the wise seek solace and the obtuse seek equal company. There is a reason why each member of the pack has a face, and the herd is faceless. Lemuria knew this because Lemuria had told them.

Steve:

Remaining in Atlantis and Lemuria, you have told us that Atlanteans were fastidious about keeping records and information, this is one of the things that they are renowned for and being that precise with any information, near enough is never good enough.

This omission becomes a big issue. We know that to begin with Atlantis and Lemuria had some form of cooperative arrangement, and he's already said that in an early answer. Then Atlantis no longer had any further contact. But there's no official reason given for severing relations except that no one was allowed to go to Lemuria, but no reason was ever given, and that's just not the way they do things.

This is a monumental separation of the two great world powers, and it really should be recorded in considerable detail. What actually happened?

To begin with I'm not dismissing the credentials or wisdom of any other Elder we've worked with. I believe they're all highly evolved elders, but Karno was different. He just lived a different way. While Kano existed beside a whitefella society, he was never a part of it. He created magic, disappeared, talked to animals, called up eagles and hawks-all things we cannot do today. Was Kano living like the ancient Lemurians of the highest level? Is that the way they lived?.

I need a bit more clarification and I know Mezreth has answered this, but nonetheless I'll ask anyway. You said earlier that Lemuria was the spiritual wand of the planet of which others were allowed to visit but never stay. Why did others, including Atlanteans need to visit Lemuria?

Mezreth:

Lemuria greets visitors through her law of judgment. It can take a day or a thousand lifetimes, but all are ultimately judged. Make no mistake, Lemurians did not make this choice. They were mere speakers of the land. Lemuria understood something beyond what her guests could see. She read the book and cast her choice in favour for the events to come or against. Never forget Lemuria, she still judges.

If a soul was once Lemurian or Atlantean, they will forever be recognized as such. However, unlike Atlantia, Lemuria is still here and speaks only to those who listen. Atlantean souls have lost their connection to their land but can attain solace through a memory of the clock that can be turned back for the distant future of today. That is why I have hope. There are thousands of Atlanteans to one Lemurian.

Atlantia was a clock, but Atlanteans were deaf to the ticking. The Lemurians could hear it and they saw how deaf Atlanteans were and the Lemurians desperately sympathized.

Steve:

It could have been they tried and tried and then realized one day that they just couldn't be helped. It could be they gave it their best shot. It's a bit like today. If you tried that today, you'd have a whole lot of trouble with any group in control listening, just like it was back then.

What spiritual function does Uluru perform in sustaining this Lemurian legacy? Why was Uluru the location where ceremonies were held recently that will transform everything?

I want to talk about the rings of Lemuria simply because they are an accurate reflection of where Lemuria was, and still is. They are of massive diameter. They're not made for normal people or normal fingers.

The question is, the rings are of a massive diameter, were they made for giants and what actually happens when these rings were worn by them?

Then it could have been passed on to people of a lower height and stature as long as they were evolved and spiritual. I put it on, and I wear it as often as I can, but I have to be careful because it is so big and wide it will fall off my finger. Of all the deeds, aspirations and intentions of Lemurians, what most impressed Mezreth and why?

Mezreth:

Uluru is the soul of Lemuria. There's the future you now inhabit, and it is where it all began and will all end.

Those rings were made for those who embodied Lemuria. They were parted and scattered across the landscapes. Each piece becoming greater than what was before and the Atlanteans realized this.

The one thing countless cultures have failed to achieve (and this is countless cultures across the board, not just on humans.) The Lemurians never took the power of face from the land. Instead, they nurtured it, tended it until it became its own face in turn, the land gave them its power.

Steve:

They become the face of the land. So that's the difference. And, of course, I've made this point often that once a culture starts to fight against nature, there is a heavy price to pay as it must lose everything. And there's such a difference because there's no nurturing, there's no ceremony. And I'm sure that the Lemurians, like the Original people of Australia, gave ceremony to the land. And that's what we're learning here.

That also means that we're falling into that Atlantean trap again. We've been told Aliens did live on Earth in Atlantis for a considerable time. Did the same living arrangements exist on the Lemuria and why did these cease?

Atlantis fell on its sword through its own mistakes and loss of direction. In Lemuria, there were not the same mistakes or loss of direction. So, the question still remains, did other negative circumstances prevail because even if it was spread out in a network, the geographical network disappeared.

Mezreth:

All visitors had to pass through laws and into the belly of Lemuria. The Lemurians, who had been there for countless millennia, were still seen as visitors. Yet their judgment allowed them to stay and learn.

Lemuria is still here and making choices either for the ending or against the ending of the book.

Transcript Eleven
Chapter 22

Steve:

Are there actually yowies in our bush, because the scientists still say they do not exist; mind you, the scientists tell us a lot of other things I do not believe. Anyway, if they are wrong, are they from here or off-world in origin?

If they are real, what are their intentions and why are they so wary of adult humans?

We took Harries Carrol, who is featured on the TV show Bondi Rescue, into country at Kariong. His six-year-old son, Billy, came with him. Billy saw a little hairy man watching him, he told his father that he could see a little yowie, and he did. All Original keepers of Old Lore believe they exist also. And they are right, and if so, what are their skills and talents and why is it they are so drawn to play with, and even kidnap for a time, human children? There are actually stories about them taking children for two or three days and then putting them back. So, what can he tell us about these little ones? Are they the same group as the yowies or different?

One part of his opening commentary claims that when humans came here, they were fully evolved with seven senses, more empathetic and aware than we are today. We were at our pinnacle then and we've been falling backwards ever since. This is open contradiction with the experts who claim we were far more primitive and duller, and slowly evolved to where we are now, the pinnacle of progress. Who was right, and if it is Slater, why does he use the term "we came here'?"

Mezreth:

They are the last remaining pure Elementals. They are what you could have been, they are wild but as aware as you. The forests are their cities, and the trees are their skyscrapers, but they see and hear what threatens their homes every single day, and it is not children. Over millennia, they have been forced to adapt to your growing presence; despite their ferocity, they are aware they are not the apex predator of the Earth. That horrid crown is on humans.

Those beings are as clever as adults, but their hearts are as children. If you are gifted to their frequency, they will welcome you if they are confident in your intent. Like their larger and more potent cousins, the little men are also aware of the viciousness of grown men. However, the little men know this wasn't always so. They aspire to bond with fledgelings, in the hopes they can subdue this terrifying aspect of men.

You were never fully evolved, but you are not entirely made by the hands of nature.

Steve:

Let's get back to the stage we are at now, the mess we are trying to fix things up. There's a particular moment in time, the global change taking place that is full of hope and redemption, but I heard something Mezreth said last time that made me a little worried. He said that for every Lemurian soul incarnate right now, there are thousands of Atlantean souls present and on world. Knowing that the oncoming changes heavily relies upon Lemurian wisdom and aspirations, isn't the sheer bulk of those with Atlantean leanings and potential failings too much of a hurdle to overcome in these times? My thinking is, if it is well over a thousand to one, it would sound like the odds aren't great to orchestrate the change when you've got such a massive percentage of people that have no empathy or familiarity with the presence of Lemuria, so how do we get around that one?

While we are speaking about that change, I wanted to change sources and go completely left field by quoting from a song by 'Yes', which was written and sung by John Anderson. There are two lines I feel are very relevant, "We began at the first spring, that the promise will come when the promise is made." Now, I've always have found those two lines fascinating. What is the promise, and can you describe what that first spring is?

Mezreth:

You know now, why it failed before. History does not have to repeat itself. The east and west are not superior over the other; if either one overcomes the other, another failure will be your future. What we hope for is seeing the marriage of east and west, both must compromise for the sake of each other.

The promise is the answer to the question of why you came here at this time. To see spring, you must endure the winter; you have never seen spring, you came close once before, and maybe you will see it this time.

Steve:

While at Uluru, Sarah had a vision that while the UFO hovered over Uluru during the ceremony, and for anyone that is not sure about her authenticity or they think such talk is nonsense, go to our web site; there is an article where we filmed it. And honestly, once you see the film of Uluru exploding into sheet of intense light blanketing the sky and another video of what could only be a UFO slowly flying above the rock at the same time, you won't so readily question Sarah's honesty or sanity. This is what she said; she sensed and saw a powerful feminine energy or entity leave the ship and merge into the big red rock. That was a bit of a shock then but certainly has visual backing. My question for Mezreth is what is it that actually happened, what did the lens see when the white light burst forth from the red rock?

Let's stay down this track a bit, because as we get closer to the change that's ahead, I'm going to be re-stating questions asked earlier, but I'll add something to it. In that semi-repetitive vain I partially asked this before, but not specifically in these words: Is the Earth the only planet that's heartbeat vibration, which is measured through the Shuman resonance, is increasing so rapidly?

Mezreth:

Humans are not the only ones that have hummed to Uluru. We bond with you in many ways; not just with speakers. We want you to see the universe from where we are.

No, far from the only one.

Steve:

That does lead on to a question about whether that's by design or by accident; but I'll ask that another time. We get reports all the time, from people about the Shuman resonance and how often it is accelerating to readings never seen or sensed before. Whereas before it would shoot up every now and then, every couple of months there'll be a little peak; now it's nearly a daily or weekly event where it's really just ramping up constantly. And I'm wondering what is the immediate impact of the huge increase, I'm not talking about down the line and what it leads up to, what is the immediate impact this has on human beings living on this planet now? Is it positive, negative or both?

So, I embrace the chaos, I think it's a great idea, because out of chaos comes change. And the change is coming, real soon. As the Schuman residence keeps ramping up this change, will that see the so-called junk DNA and the brain running at 15% capacity both spark up if the soul is willing and committed? But what happens to those amongst us who are not ready for this redemptive chaos?

Mezreth:

The turmoil is akin to what happened before, but to see spring, you need to understand how to overcome it forever. This is the best way for each individual to have this foundation laid. Without this, you will lack the wisdom for future challenges.

The ones who go on will be changed for the better as one may imagine but there will come a worse time, remember the cost of arrogance! Humility is the lantern in the dark. Yes, you are open to vulnerability, but you will be seen as true and trusted. Knowing and embracing your strengths and weaknesses may bring you higher. But you asked what happens to those without lanterns: they remain untouched, unseen, and blind in the dark. The cruellest karma that can befall a soul is nothing; they don't' grow, they don't change, they linger in life, but they are already dead.

Lea's Final Comments

This book was made not for me, nor for Steven, or even for Mezreth. Our names are irrelevant, our singular lives are temporary, what matters are the discussions pressed into these pages. My trust in Mezreth is not because he's an ancient being from another world, but because his sayings and perceptions were relevant to me and all our everyday lives. He was there when I threw tantrums and when I wept with joy. When I asked questions, he would ensure I took the time to learn more about the subject before he would add to it. Only when my ego was beaten down, that was when he would speak. Everything I learnt was earned, and overtime, he earned my trust – as well as I earned his.

Conclusion

Every word, syllable and punctuation mark in this book are all predicated around a huge leap of faith. There are only two sides to this report, either Lea is fabricating or imagining her interaction with Mezreth, or she is telling the truth. There is no other alternative, it has to be one or the other.

The critical empirical vacuum in this account that is missing in action is that we have no supporting photograph, archaeology, or tangible proof. It all comes down to our assurances and that of Mezreth's responses and whether they are separate conversations, or are they merely lies created to satisfy our greed or need to deceive and mislead?

In determining which path is more likely we believe the answer lays within what he said. It all comes down to the depth and breadth of response, the wisdom of his observations and the knowledge gained that underpins his answers. I would ask the reader if he or she knows anyone who could equal or better what Mezreth offers up, if they have ever read a book that canvasses every aspect of our existence and that of the planet and Cosmos as well? If that is the case it may be possible that although Lea did not apply herself at school, she has an IQ score that can be measured in the hundreds and is capable of understanding and knowing literally everything.

If the reader is prepared to accept the possibility that what Lea is relaying is genuine, there still remains an issue in relation to timing. Quite simply it could be asked, why now, why share the knowledge of the ages at this particular time? Why not earlier, perhaps at the turn of nineteenth century, just before two World Wars and countless minor skirmishes, or maybe go further back coinciding with the ministry of Jesus, Buddha, Allah or earlier prophets?

The answer to those lays within the last category, which deals with the Earthly ascension ceremony at Uluru. Before that seminal global rite of passage was sung and danced into activation, life on this planet was merely a prelude to the main event. The main reason why Mezreth decided to share knowledge of so many hidden secrets is due to both this ceremony which inaugurated the beginning of Earth increasing in magic and energy levels, and just as importantly the accompanying acceleration in "strife" of which Mezreth conceded is rarely matched anywhere else. Such is the magnitude and depth of this negative force, he felt compelled to offer guidance and directions forward.

The problem faced here is that the expected equilibrium between good and evil is no longer present. Those who manipulate and control have the reins and podium. The media, commerce and politics serve the elite, powerful and obscenely rich. Right now, this is a world of warfare, pandemics, terrorism and unemployment and the light at the end of the tunnel is barely flickering. When this ceremony at Uluru was about to be enacted we reached out to literally every media outlet, and one reporter from the ABC responded and was adamant he could get news of this broadcasted, but that all changed when a directive from 'up high' made it clear nothing concerning this ceremony was going to air.

It is because of this dire situation where the truth is hidden or censored that Mezreth set about slowly but surely compiling a set of guidelines and destinations through a second and third party. Now if he had landed a spaceship at Parliament House at Canberra and handed over a book with all he advised and recommended, that would be more dramatic, simpler and would compel many to listen and consider. But such a covert action is a direct intervention (which has been agreed should never happen), whereas this way people can just dismiss this all as a dishonest ruse and walk away. Afterall the millions who joined in the ceremony had no empirical proof, in fact we always said we were not convinced the ceremony would even take place. Those who became part of this global ceremony directed at Uluru did so knowing it was couched in maybes. This is what this book does, we have no film, alien devices or photographs to present, just what an Alien told an unknown someone who is not a celebrity, sports star or rich tycoon.

So, this all comes down to Mezreth laying out the inner foundations as to why we exist and the challenges each human resident on this planet must resolve, now. If accepting and committing to what he suggests then the chances that person will be part of, rather than apart from, the eminent increase in Earthly transformation. Everything here is based around each person having free will to choose or discard, that is the way it has always been. But right now, there is one cardinal difference. In previous incarnations your errors were transferred over to your next incarnation on Earth to address, correct or ignore. But this time around there are long-term consequences in that what you do right now and in the days to come before the change, determines where you go next, and for many it will be anywhere else but Earth.

But there is one final catch in what Mezreth is offering. The ceremony did succeed, and this sacred planet has begun the cleansing process, that was always guaranteed if the numbers exceeded a set level, which they did. However, what was never made clear, but undeniably hinted at by many including us, was the 'when' part of this equation. We will go in more details soon, but the time of transformation has been extended, it is no longer applicable as it was intended to be counted in years, but it has now been deemed to be both wiser and more prudent to extend the collective length of our stay of either execution or redemption, to be numbered in decades. In the great scale of what this Earthly experiment was set to achieve, such an extension is miniscule, but for the many who sense intuitively that a major change is afoot and soon, they do need to accept it will take a bit longer and require a lot more patience and faith.

What Mezreth hopes will come to pass, is that humans on Earth have the opportunity to become citizens of not just the Earth, but the Universe. But if they look away, so too when they pass on their Earthly tenure will be cancelled and their next incarnation has to be elsewhere on a planet that is not ascending, but static and vibrating at a much lower level. It really is a matter of one or the other, and the recurring part of the choice that must be made is that each person gets to choose their destiny and residence. We believe that this book and the content within could lead towards the best choice you could ever make, or equally, you could dismiss this as fictional and mischievous, but this time around that is a decision made during a time when the consequences are immediate.

What Mezreth is revealing tells us so much about who we are, why we are here and what makes this planet so special. He has told us often that this planet offers the quickest way to advance your soul and karma, but alas that is because this planet is experiencing more "strife" than anywhere else. Well, that affliction and addiction is coming to an end, but as to actually where that leaves each current human resident is totally a personal choice. And this is where our book finishes, what comes next is your story alone and whether it is compiled here or there is all about you making the right choice now.

www.ingramcontent.com/pod-product-compliance
Lightning Source LLC
Chambersburg PA
CBHW051422290426
44109CB00016B/1397